T0316684

Cambridge Elements ≡

Elements in Politics and Society in Southeast Asia
Edited by
Edward Aspinall
Australian National University
Meredith L. Weiss
University at Albany, SUNY

CIVIL–MILITARY RELATIONS IN SOUTHEAST ASIA

Aurel Croissant
Heidelberg University

CAMBRIDGE
UNIVERSITY PRESS

CAMBRIDGE
UNIVERSITY PRESS

University Printing House, Cambridge CB2 8BS, United Kingdom

One Liberty Plaza, 20th Floor, New York, NY 10006, USA

477 Williamstown Road, Port Melbourne, VIC 3207, Australia

314–321, 3rd Floor, Plot 3, Splendor Forum, Jasola District Centre, New Delhi – 110025, India

79 Anson Road, #06–04/06, Singapore 079906

Cambridge University Press is part of the University of Cambridge.

It furthers the University's mission by disseminating knowledge in the pursuit of education, learning, and research at the highest international levels of excellence.

www.cambridge.org
Information on this title: www.cambridge.org/9781108459099
DOI: 10.1017/9781108654715

First published 2018

A catalogue record for this publication is available from the British Library.

ISBN 978-1-108-45909-9 Paperback
ISSN 2515-2998 (online)
ISSN 2515-298X (print)

Civil–Military Relations in Southeast Asia

Politics and Society in Southeast Asia

DOI: 10.1017/9781108654715
First published online: August 2018

Aurel Croissant
Heidelberg University

Abstract: *Civil–Military Relations in Southeast Asia* reviews the historical origins, contemporary patterns, and emerging changes in civil–military relations in Southeast Asia from colonial times until today. It examines what types of military organizations emerged in the late colonial period and the impact of colonial legacies and the Japanese occupation in World War II on the formation of national armies and their role in processes of achieving independence. It analyzes the long-term trajectories and recent changes of professional, revolutionary, praetorian, and neopatrimonial civil–military relations in the region. Finally, it discusses military roles in state- and nation-building; political domination, revolutions and regime transitions, and military entrepreneurship.

Keywords: military, democracy, authoritarianism, colonialism, Southeast Asia

ISBNs: 9781108459099 (PB), 9781108654715 (OC)
ISSNs: 2515-2998 (online), 2515-298X (print)

Contents

1 Introduction   1

2 Historical Origins of Civil–Military Relations   12

3 Types of Civil–Military Relations   26

4 Military Roles: Old and New   45

5 Conclusions and Outlook   60

  References   70

1 Introduction

In recent decades, many Southeast Asian countries experienced important and sometimes dramatic transformations of their political or economic structures. Between 1986 and 2002, democratically elected governments replaced authoritarian rule in the Philippines, Thailand, Indonesia, Cambodia, and Timor-Leste (Shin and Tusalem 2009). In 2010, the military in Myanmar initiated a process of gradual disengagement from day-to-day politics that led to the election of a democratic government in 2015. Following the inauguration of market-oriented economic reforms in the mid-1980s, Laos and Vietnam experienced profound socioeconomic change. Finally, opposition parties in Malaysia won a historic election victory in May 2018 and toppled the Barisan Nasional coalition, which had been in power since 1957.

Such transformations often contributed to profound shifts in the military's role in politics and society, as illustrated by the decreasing number of military-led regimes in Southeast Asia, from five in 1970 to one in 2010 (Geddes, Wright, and Frantz 2014).[1] Nevertheless, civil–military relations in the region are still diverse and feature a remarkable mix of continuity and change. For example, despite successful democratization, the Indonesian National Armed Forces (TNI) continue "to yield considerable political power" in postauthoritarian Indonesia (Mietzner 2018: 140). In the Philippines, civilian governments forged a symbiotic relationship with military elites, which allowed civilians to survive in office but enabled the Armed Forces of the Philippines (AFP) to preserve some of their authoritarian and preauthoritarian prerogatives (Croissant et al. 2013). And in Thailand, the military coups in 2006 and 2014 demonstrated that even after almost fifteen years of temporary retreat from government to barracks, military rule is a continuing danger in that country. Civil–military relations in Timor-Leste, while more stable than in the Philippines or Thailand, are also strained (Sahin and Feaver 2013). Since the general elections of July 2017 and the failed attempt to build a new coalition government, observers noticed a resurgence of "increasingly belligerent rhetoric" that is endangering political stability and the security of the population (Feijó 2018: 212). Finally, recent developments in Myanmar such as a sweeping military crackdown on the Muslim Rohingya ethnic group demonstrate that the *Bama Tatmadaw* (Burmese for "armed forces") remains a power that "state counselor" Aung San Suu Kyi cannot control (Fink 2018: 161).

Such ambiguities of civil–military interactions contrast with the seemingly prosaic routine of civil–military interactions in party-based autocracies. Most

---

[1] *Armed forces, armed services,* and *the military* are used interchangeably throughout this Element.

features of civil–military relations in Singapore, Vietnam, Laos, and Malaysia have been remarkably constant and coherent, including the undisputed predominance of the civilian sector over the military, the absence of military power centers beyond the reach of the ruling parties, and those parties' invulnerability to coups.

What explains these divergent paths? Why did different types of military organizations emerge in the late colonial and early postcolonial periods, and how did the role of new armies in the process of state- and nation-building affect civil–military relations in the new nation-states of Southeast Asia? What have been the roles and missions of Southeast Asian militaries, and how have they changed from independence until today? What types of civil–military relations emerged, and what are main factors that explain change and continuity in the interactions between soldiers, state, and society?

1.1 The Existing Scholarship

Since its inception in the 1950s, the scholarship on the interactions between soldiers, state, and society in Southeast Asia has moved in different directions. The field initially focused on the role of military elites in processes of decolonization and state-building in new nations. In the 1970s, the scholarship moved toward analyzing the origins and political practice of military rule. Since the 1990s, a new generation of studies in civil–military relations has emerged that illuminates the military's role in the breakdown of authoritarianism and how young democracies struggle with creating a military that is strong enough to fulfill its functions but is subordinate to the authority of democratically elected institutions.[2] Finally, in the 2000s, works on security-sector governance have become the most recent addition to the literature on civil–military relations in Southeast Asia. The focus on the "security sector" and the military as a provider of "human (in)security" reflects the increase in nonconventional threats in the region, such as international terrorism, organized crime, environmental degradation and pandemics, and irregular migration. Yet, compared with the rich literature on security-sector reforms in Latin America, postcommunist Europe, and Africa, the research on Southeast Asia has expanded slowly (Beeson and Bellamy 2008).

Even though the civil–military scholarship in Southeast Asia has grown, the field is still problematic in a number of ways. First, much of the recent scholarship focuses on the role of the armed forces in democratization and in changes in form and/or substance of civilian control over the military in new democracies, failing to explore civil–military relations in dictatorships, even as

---

[2] For critical reviews of these research trends, see Alagappa (2001a) and Croissant (2016).

authoritarianism remains the rule and democracy the exception in the region (Case 2015).

Second, the extraordinarily diverse nature of Southeast Asia in terms of history, demographics, culture, economy, and political systems has clearly been detrimental to the development of a more comparative research agenda. Most studies of the relationship between the soldier and the state in Southeast Asia focus only on one or two countries and operate in relative isolation from analysis of civil–military relations in other regions of the world. This means that Southeast Asian studies have contributed little to the development of theories and concepts in the general civil–military relations literature, which has focused on other developing areas such as Latin America and the Middle East. As Evan Laksmana (2008: 7) asserts, "Southeast Asian militaries [have] suffered from too little theorizing as the focus thus far has been based on area studies scholarship of military politics."

Third, studies on Indonesia, Thailand, and Myanmar dominate the civil–military relations research in Southeast Asia mainly due to the turbulences of coup politics and military rule, separatist movements, outbreaks of violence, and other upheavals that have been a persistent feature of their postindependence history. There is considerably less research on the Philippines and Vietnam and very little on the civil–military relations of smaller countries such as Cambodia, Malaysia, and Singapore, not to mention Brunei, Timor-Leste, and Laos. Often, however, generalizations for Southeast Asia as such apply only to the few "focus" cases of civil–military relations and not to the rest of the region. In fact, a key difference between Southeast Asia, on the one hand, and Latin America, postcommunist Europe, North Africa, and the Middle East, on the other, is the lack of a single Southeast Asian pattern of civil–military relations. Latin America, with few exceptions, experienced the rise of military rule in the 1960s and 1970s and a wave of transitions from military governments to democratic regimes in the 1980s and 1990s (Pion-Berlin and Martinez 2017). The relationship between the party and the military in all communist regimes in Europe before 1990 followed the Soviet model of party supremacy, based on an effective mixture of control mechanisms, elite fusion, and co-optation of military leaders into the party's prime decision-making bodies (Croissant and Kuehn 2015). And in the Middle East and North Africa, the military has played a central role in almost all authoritarian republics (Koehler 2016). In contrast, the countries of Southeast Asia represent what is arguably the most diverse collection of civil–military relations of any region in the world. Consequently, we have very little in the way of comparative typologies of civil–military relations in Southeast Asia.

1.2 Conceptual Framework

The key concept used in this Element is *civil–military relations*. This term encompasses the entire range of interactions between the military and civilian society at every level (Feaver 1999: 211). However, political science has typically adopted a more narrow focus on the structures, processes, and outcomes of the interactions between the political system, on the one hand, and the armed forces, on the other (Croissant and Kuehn 2015: 258). In this regard, the term *civilians* encompasses all organizations, institutions, and actors that make, implement, and monitor political decisions and substantive policies. It not only includes the state institutions of the core executive, legislative, and judicial branches of government but also nonstate political actors such as political parties, interest groups, social movements, and associations of civil society, as well as international actors such as foreign governments, international financial institutions, and nongovernmental organizations (NGOs).

The definition of *military* used in this study refers to "that organization, or group of organizations, which is permanently established by constitutional law, enjoys a monopoly over certain categories of weapons and equipment, and is responsible for the constrained application of violence or coercive force to eliminate or deter any thing or body that is considered to threaten the existence of the nation-state" (Edmonds 1988: 26). What is excluded from this definition are nonstate armed groups, such as guerilla armies, vigilantes, and terrorist organizations. Also not part of this definition are other core security actors that the policy-oriented scholarship describes as the "security sector," such as police, paramilitary forces, intelligence services, coast or border guards, civil defense forces, and government militias (Edmunds 2012).

The fundamental issue in civil–military relations is how to create and preserve a military that is subordinate to political control but is also effective and efficient (Feaver 1999). There is no agreement on what exactly civilian control over the military entails, nor how this concept should be measured. However, in recent years, scholars have advanced conceptions that share two fundamental assumptions (Croissant et al. 2013; Pion-Berlin and Martinez 2017). First, civilian control is about the political power of the military relative to the nonmilitary political actors. Second, and related, political–military relations can best be understood as a continuum ranging from full civilian control to complete military dominance over the political system.

In this understanding, *civilian control* is a particular form of distribution of the authority to make political decisions in which civilian leaders (either democratically elected or autocratically selected) have the authority to decide on national politics and its implementation. While civilians may delegate the implementation of certain policies to the military, the latter has no decision-making power outside of those areas specifically defined by governments. In contrast, if a government is subordinate to and exists only at the tolerance of a military that retains the right to intervene when it perceives a crisis, a regime is effectively under military tutelage. Finally, the term *military control* shall be reserved for situations in which the military controls government, either through collegial bodies representing the officer corps (*military regime*) or because decision-making power is concentrated in the hands of a single military officer (*military strongman rule*; Geddes, Wright, and Frantz 2014).

Western models of civil–military relations presume that a military's primary mission is to defend the state against external threats. However, in developing countries and postcolonial states, militaries often fulfill a variety of other roles, including nation-building, economic development, and regime protection. This Element distinguishes four such roles and missions (Croissant, Eschenauer, and Kamerling 2017; Croissant and Eschenauer 2018)[3]:

1. **State- and Nation-Building.** In this role, militaries act as transmitters of nationalism, diffusing anticolonialism and national ideologies among local populations and becoming agents in the early creation of large-scale socio-political organizations. In particular, military conscription is an instrument of military-based state- and nation-building. Besides having a socializing function, military state- and nation-builders regularly steer political agendas and engage in economic and administrative activities.

2. **The Exercise and Organization of Political Domination.** Military-as-ruler constitutes the most obvious and dominant role a military can fulfill in the exercise and organization of political power. The military fulfills the role of ruler if military officers dominate the regime coalition and steer the political process – either overtly or behind a civilianized facade. Military-as-supporter, in contrast, does not rule but instead supports and assists the political leadership in exercising and organizing political power. By deterring political opposition, military supporters ensure the regime's survival and become one of its stabilizing pillars. In return, the military receives concessions, for example, impunity from prosecution for human rights violations, autonomy in its own internal affairs, or other political prerogatives. While ruling militaries possess governing qualities themselves, militaries as supporters exert extensive influence on those holding political power (Croissant, Eschenauer, and Kamerling 2017). Finally, a military can assume a role as the servant of the civilian authorities. Here

---

[3] This differentiation does not assume a linear or evolutionary succession of military roles. Instead, roles may merge, alternate, or overlap.

the military might provide security for the regime, but it does not autonomously decide the extent of its engagement and does not exert either formal or informal veto rights in political affairs.

3. **Regime Transitions.** Regime transitions sometimes start with mass mobilization. However, military roles in situations of anti-incumbent mass contention vary considerably across dictatorships. Some militaries defend the incumbent government against mass protests, whereas others side with the opposition or organize a coup d'état. The specific role the military plays during nonviolent revolutions – defender, defector, or coup plotter – is key to the immediate outcome. However, military institutions can also be important actors in transitions to democracy that occur without mass mobilization (i.e., transitions initiated from above or through negotiations between government and opposition). As Felipe Agüero (1998) asserts, the stronger the military's influence is during the transition, the more it can maintain its prerogatives and stifle postauthoritarian politics.

4. **Economic Development and Commercial Activities.** Despite the fact that military leaders usually make statements of intention to modernize and develop the nation and improve its standard of living on coming into power, the nature and results of the military's role in economic development vary from country to country and especially between autocratically governed states. The role of the military in the national economy is likely to be a function of the relationship of the military to the political authorities. While active participation of the military in commercial activities can have different economic consequences, it often negatively affects military effectiveness.

Furthermore, building on Amos Perlmutter's idea of general types of military organizations in modern nation-states, this Element identifies four distinct types of civil–military relations (Croissant and Kuehn 2018). These are not mutually exclusive categories; there can be hybrid cases that contain characteristics of two or more types.

1. **Professional Civil–Military Relations.** Under professional civil–military relations, civilian and military spheres of autonomy and responsibility are clearly separated. The army (although it has legitimate political interests) does not intervene in the decision-making activities of the government and other political organizations that are not aligned with the military. That is, governments in such regimes exercise full political control over their militaries.

2. **Revolutionary Political–Military Relations.** As Perlmutter (1977: 13) notes, the revolutionary military also "manifests a strong propensity

to succumb to political influence." Yet, in this second type of political–military relations, the revolutionary movement or party does not emphasize the marginalization of the revolutionary military from political affairs. Rather, the revolutionary military is political by definition, and the structures of the ruling political organization interpenetrate the armed forces, which serve as an instrument of mobilization and regime security for the revolutionary political party (Perlmutter 1977: 13–14). Although the relationship between the soldier and the party can change over time, revolutionary political–military relations are generally characterized by a *symbiosis* of military and party elites. To ensure the convergence of interests between party and military elites, military leaders are co-opted into the party apparatus (Perlmutter and LeoGrande 1982).

3. **Praetorian Political–Military Relations.** This third type emerges in countries with low levels of political institutionalization and a lack of sustained mass support for civilian political structures. Cultural, societal, and political circumstances make the use of military force to settle political disagreements likely. This leads to the rise and persistence of the *praetorian state*, in which the military dominates key political structures and institutions (Perlmutter 1974: 4). The army frequently intervenes in the government, acting either as an arbitrator, controlling affairs behind the scenes through a chosen civilian agent, or as an actual ruler (Perlmutter 1974: 8–11).

4. **Neopatrimonial Political–Military Relations.** In this type, a single leader dominates both the political regime structures and the military. As Geddes (2003: 51) explains, "[t]he leader may be an officer and has created a party to support himself but neither the military nor the party exercises independent decision-making power insulated from the whims of the ruler." In the neopatrimonial type, the military serves as another element in the leader's toolbox of authoritarian control instruments to protect him or her from both popular revolt and insider coups. Simultaneously, the military is a franchise system for the ruler in which officers pursuing career opportunities and financial benefits must seek access to the dictator's patronage system. Military officers hold positions in the military organization with powers that are formally defined, but they gain access to their position of power based on personal loyalty to the ruler; they exercise those powers, so far as they can, as a form not of public service but of private property and because it pleases the ruler. Ultimately, the importance of good connections with the ruler and his or her entourage and individual rent-seeking trump military expertise, corporate interests, and revolutionary commitment. Military behavior is correspondingly devised to display a personal interest or status rather than to perform an official, professional, or revolutionary function.

Types of political–military relations and military roles covariate but are not synonymous. For example, different roles of military in state- and nation-building, in political domination, and as economic actors coexist with more than one type (Table 1).

A final remark concerns the relationship between political regimes and types of political–military relations. Although the empirical realities to which they refer are more or less tightly interwoven, they constitute analytically distinct concepts. While military authoritarianism by definition aligns with praetorian political–military relations, highly personalist dictatorships can have either neopatrimonial or praetorian militaries. A revolutionary military requires, by definition, a revolutionary party. Therefore, it is only found in single-party dictatorships. However, most dictators form parties to support their rule, but not all ruling parties are revolutionary. Hence one-party and multiparty authoritarianism can coexist with different forms of political–military relations, ranging from revolutionary to praetorian or neopatrimonial and even professional. Finally, professional political–military relations are a logical prerequisite for consolidated liberal democracies. This is not so in new and unconsolidated democracies, where the historical legacies of the authoritarian period often include a praetorian or neopatrimonial military, and military officers sometimes play an important part in the transition from authoritarian rule.

1.3 Argument and Plan of the Element

In order to analyze civil–military relations in Southeast Asia, this Element takes a comparative historical perspective. With other works in the tradition of comparative historical analysis, it shares "a concern with causal analysis, an emphasis on process over time, and the use of systematic and contextualized comparison" (Mahoney and Rueschmeyer 2003: 10). To understand why divergent paths of civil–military interaction have emerged, remained constant, or changed, it is argued that four causal factors are particularly relevant: (1) legacies of colonial rule and Japanese occupation during World War II, (2) the mode of transition from colonial rule to independence and the role of coercion, (3) the particular threat environment during the early years of state-formation and nation-building, and (4) the strength of political parties and the type of civilian elite structure.

1. **Legacies of Colonial Rule and Japanese Occupation.** Other than the Kingdom of Siam (since 1939, Thailand), all nations of Southeast Asia experienced Western colonial rule for an extended period. Shortly after independence – and sometimes even before – all new nations except North Vietnam created facsimiles of a Western military establishment. The ranks

Table 1 Military Roles and Types of Political–Military Relations

Military role	Types of civil–military relations			
	Professional	**Revolutionary**	**Praetorian**	**Neopatrimonial**
State- and nation-building	Marginal	Subsidiary	Primary	Marginal
Political domination	Military as servant	Military as supporter	Military as ruler	Military as supporter
Revolutions and regime transitions	Subsidiary	Subsidiary	Dominant	Indeterminate
Economy	Marginal	Subsidiary	Indeterminate	Indeterminate

of the officer corps were often dominated by men of relatively young age who came from a variety of backgrounds, including colonial and anti-Japanese armies, Japanese-trained levies and irregular units, and political activists. Different backgrounds, generational conflicts, and interservice rivalries often created internal fissures and factional struggles that became major sources of political instability (Hoadley 1975: 152). Legacies of colonial rule and the Japanese occupation structured the shape of civil–military relations in the immediate postwar period and in some cases until today.

2. **Modes of Decolonization and the Role of Coercion.** Different modes of achieving independence – either through revolutionary struggle or through peaceful transition – also had important consequences for the evolution of postcolonial civil–military relations because military establishments that played a special role in processes of decolonization, nation-building, and state-formation felt empowered to demand special privileges from civilian governments. Furthermore, in some countries it was the military that was the most advanced and powerful state institution and that, in light of weak civilian administrations and failing state bureaucracies, became an important agent of modernization and social change. Consequently, the militaries' roles and missions diversified and expanded over time.

3. **Threat Environments.** In addition to legacies of colonial rule and Japanese occupation and the manner in which countries achieved independence, whether the political leaders of the new nations were challenged by communal insurgencies also strongly influenced the emerging types of civil–military relations. Where the military played a prominent role in suppressing communal unrest, Asian militaries subsequently mythologized their role as creator-guardians of the state and nation. Where civilian governments had to rely heavily on the military's coercive and organizational capabilities to ensure their hold on power, the officer corps became a major source of political influence and administrative ability. In this scenario, armies acted as transmitters of nationalism, diffusing national ideologies and anticolonialism among the populace at critical junctures; they also became agents in the early creation of large-scale sociopolitical organizations. In contrast, the future political influence of soldiers would be weaker when the military had no meaningful role to play in putting down class-based or ethnic insurgencies.

4. **Political Parties and Elite Structures.** Historical legacies and structural contexts alone cannot explain why military rule prevailed in Indonesia, South Vietnam, and Burma but not in Malaysia, North Vietnam, and Singapore. The road from colonial repression, liberation struggle, or armed insurgency to military praetorianism was often short, but it was not unavoidable. Rather, civilian elite cohesion and party politics were other

important causal factors. The argument here is that in the latter group of countries, consensually unified civilian elites and strong party institutions generated conditions that minimized both the incentives for politicians to pull the military into the domain of government and the opportunity for military leaders to push into civilian politics (Slater 2010b). The prerequisites for the military's marginal political role were the formation of relatively strong nonmilitary political organizations and civilian institutions still under colonial rule, the exclusion of members of the military from the political sphere, limited military capabilities, and the co-optation of key elites through political parties, ruling coalitions, and regime institutions. In contrast, weak institutionalization of civilian political organizations and the lack of sustained support for political structures led civilian political groups to rely heavily on the military's coercive and organizational powers to establish state structures and enforce the political elites' claim to power. This empowered militaries vis-à-vis the civilian elites and ultimately led to the emergence of praetorian militaries.

Although this Element emphasizes structural foundations, historical legacies, and path-dependent processes to explain patterns of long-term civil–military relations, this is not to say that military roles or political–military relations remained static. As Muthiah Alagappa (2001a: 433) notes, there have been changes in Asian civil–military relations, especially during and after transitions to democracy – itself often endogenous to structural changes – that led to "a reduction in the political power, influence and role of the military." But past actions, developments, and legacies constrain present choices; the potential of change in civil–military relations becomes far more difficult as actors become entrenched in distinctive development paths.

Of course, political leadership matters, and the concrete state of civil–military relations always is an outcome of the interaction between military and nonmilitary actors, who each have their own set of interests and act according to them. Yet, even in situations of regime change and political revolutions, political actors are constrained by the conditions that they inherit from events and structures that occurred previously (Croissant et al. 2013). In fact, authoritarian and preauthoritarian legacies of civil–military relations such as particular military roles, the existence of well-established mechanisms of political control of the military (or lack thereof), the political privileges and prerogatives that military elites carved out during a transition process, and deeply entrenched patterns of civil–military elite conflict or convergence have had a strong impact on processes of institutionalizing changes in civil–military relations after the (temporary) transition from authoritarian to democratic governments not only in Southeast Asia but also in other regions, such as Latin America (Agüero 1998) and postcommunist Europe (Barany 2012). Accordingly, Croissant et al. (2013) have suggested an understanding of military reforms in situations of (democratic) regime change (or lack thereof) as the outcome of a complex interplay between structural factors and political agency. Even though the successful crafting of military and defense reforms in new democracies ultimately depends on the ability of civilians to "break up" military prerogatives remaining from the preauthoritarian and authoritarian periods, the environmental context presents those actors with resources and opportunities.

The rest of this Element approaches its topic by combining three perspectives. First, it brings into focus the role of military officers in democracies and nondemocracies, thus filling a gap in the literature on the Southeast Asian region. Second, it seeks to identify and explain the empirical (versus normative) elements of the actual relationship between the soldier and the state in Southeast Asia. Third, it offers contextualized and systematic comparisons of all eleven Southeast Asian countries that prioritize the larger states in the region but also reviews the smaller nations.

The remainder of this Element proceeds as follows. Section 2 examines the legacies of colonial armies and the Japanese occupation in World War II on the formation of national militaries and how the role of military forces in processes of achieving independence and guarding the nation-state against communal or class-based rebellions structured the shape of postwar civil–military relations in the region. Section 3 employs the typology of civil–military relations introduced earlier to analyze the long-term trajectories and recent changes in the relationship between soldiers and the state in Southeast Asia. Section 4 relies on the previously introduced differentiation of four military roles to make a comparative analysis of the different roles of Southeast Asian militaries. Section 5 provides conclusions and a discussion of future prospects of Southeast Asian civil–military relations.

2 Historical Origins of Civil–Military Relations

This section examines how modern military organizations emerged in Southeast Asia, discusses their role in achieving independence and in guarding the new nation-states against class-based or ethnic insurgencies, and assesses the military's track record in early postwar regime formation.

2.1 Colonial Armies (and the Deviant Case of Thailand)

European colonialism expanded in Southeast Asia from the 1510s to the 1900s, with Western colonial power reaching its apex between 1870 and

1914 (Osborne 1990). Colonial rule appeared in different forms, and the extent of coercion used to control local populations varied over space and time. However, European powers in Southeast Asia always lacked the numbers to field a full army of Western troops to garrison their colonial possessions. Consequently, colonial powers recruited large parts of their colonial forces from within their non-Western territories (Hack and Rettig 2009a: 4). Initially, most colonial powers used ethnoreligious policies of selected recruitment to some extent. The careful recruitment of politically reliable individuals could include, for instance, "Asiatic" minorities from Indonesia's "Outer Islands" and the "Frontier Areas" of Burma or recruits from other colonial territories, for example, Sikhs and Gurkhas from India. By the 1910s, however, the expanding colonial armies increasingly had to rely on the local majority populations for recruitment in order to keep abreast of increasing domestic and international threats. This meant, for example, more recruits from the Javanese population for the army in the Dutch Indies and more Vietnamese soldiers in Indochina (Hack and Rettig 2009).

In Burma, which the British had conquered in three wars between 1824 and 1886, applying the principles of ethnic differentiation to recruitment of troops resulted in the dominant ethnic group of Burmans (also known as Bamar) accounting for only 12 percent of the indigenous troops in 1931. Despite the increase in numbers of Burmans after 1937 when Burma was made a distinct colony, the army remained very much an ethnic minority force. In 1941, Burmans accounted for 23.7 percent of the total military personnel, compared with 35 percent Karen, 15.7 percent Chin, and 10.6 percent Kachin soldiers (Callahan 2005: 36–42).

In the Indochinese Union, comprising Cambodia, Laos, and Vietnam, the French formed various indigenous units, among which the *garde indigène* and *garde civil de Cochinchine* were most important (Lee 1971: 42). These forces were officered by the French themselves, while enlisted personal were mostly Vietnamese, or "Khiet" (Womack 2009). Under mounting pressure from Japan in the late 1930s, the French Ministry of Colonies sought to build a Vietnamese national army that would fight against the Japanese if necessary (Lee 1971: 43). However, these prewar efforts failed, and the only lasting effect was to provide tens of thousands of Vietnamese with some degree of military training, "a result which was later to benefit the Viet Minh [the communist forces] and the other anti-French forces who joined in the post-war struggle for Vietnamese independence" (Hoadley 1975: 68).

The situation in the Philippines, Malaya, and Brunei contrasts starkly with that of the Dutch Indies, Burma, and Indochina. The "native" component of the US colonial army in the Philippines had its origin in the Philippine–American

War of 1899–1902. Recruitment of local soldiers for the Philippine Scout companies and the paramilitary Philippine Constabulary (PC), the nation's main law enforcement agency, began in 1901, first in order to combat the Filipino revolutionaries and later to subdue Muslim rebels in Mindanao (Meixsel 2009). In accordance with the Tydings-McDuffie Act, the Philippine Army was officially created in December 1935. The PC became the constabulary division of the army, creating a tradition of military command of the police that prevailed until 1991. In December 1941, the bulk of American forces stationed in the Philippines were native forces, who were far more effectively integrated into the US Army than native troops in British-held Malaya and Singapore (Hanson 2017: 342–44).

The British reluctantly increased recruitment of the Malays, leading to the formation of the Malay Regiment in 1933. Due to potential Malay resistance, however, the colonial authorities avoided recruiting Chinese, who constituted a third of the population on the peninsula, in larger numbers. For the Malay elites, who had pressured the colonial authorities to establish a native armed force, the Malay Regiment became a symbol of Malay culture and self-confidence (Nathan and Govindasamy 2001: 261). Nonetheless, the share of Malays in the colonial army remained at less than 10 percent of the troops stationed on the Malay Peninsula in early December 1941 (Hack 2009: 245).

Thailand was the only Southeast Asian state to remain independent during the colonial period. The reforms of King Mongkut (r. 1851–68) laid the groundwork for a modern Thai military. In 1852, the Royal Siamese Army (since 1939, the Royal Thai Armed Forces) became a permanent and European-trained force (Chambers 2013: 108). In 1887, King Chulalongkorn (r. 1868–1910) brought the army, the King's Guard, and smaller military organizations under the unified command of a Military Affairs Department. An army cadet academy was established, and ranks, positions, training, and pay were standardized (Somvichian 1969). In 1897, the practice of recruiting commoners by competitive examination for study abroad was instituted. In 1902, universal conscription was introduced, and the army was greatly expanded (Hoadley 1975: 11).

Despite these reforms, the control of the armed forces remained in the hands of the king, and top military posts were reserved for royal princes. Nonetheless, a new group of commoner-class officers emerged in both the civil and military hierarchies during the first two decades of the twentieth century. The absolute power of the palace and its reliance on traditional aristocratic elites clashed with the interests of new elites in the civilian and military bureaucracies. Rising tensions between new and old elites and the fallout of the Great Depression of 1929 finally culminated in a coup d'état by a group of military officers and bureaucrats against King Prajadhipok (Rama VII) on June 24, 1932 (Wyatt 1984: 239–41). The 1932 coup resulted in a drastic shift of the social bases of elite recruitment and entrenched the army's budgetary and personal dominance vis-à-vis the navy (Samudavanija 1971; Lissak 1976).

Most important, the overthrow of the absolute monarchy in 1932 led to the emergence of a "bureaucratic polity" (Riggs 1966), in which the state bureaucracy became the primary arena of political rivalry for parcels of state control between civilian bureaucrats and military elites (Connors 2003: 11). Personal relations with senior officers, the types of affiliated corps, and interservice rivalry had been significant drivers of military factionalism before 1932, but when the army became the dominant branch and organizational changes improved the "jointness" of the three branches, membership in a class at the military academy became the main distinguishing feature (Chambers 2010).

2.2 The Impact of Japanese Occupation

The Japanese occupation of Southeast Asia in World War II had a powerful impact on the region. Within six months of the attack on Pearl Harbor on December 7, 1941, Japanese forces overran Burma, Malaya, Singapore, Borneo, the Philippines, and Indonesia. The Japanese Imperial Army and Fleet threatened British India and Allied supply lines to Australia. While technically allies of Japan, French Indochina and Thailand had to accept the deployment of Japanese troops. By mid-1943, however, the tide had turned against the Japanese, and by mid-1944, Tokyo's defeat was only a matter of time.

While most colonial troops remained loyal to their colonial masters (Hack and Rettig 2009b: 54), a mixture of local initiatives and Japanese political and strategic considerations led to the creation of pro-Japanese militias and volunteer armies throughout Southeast Asia (Lebra 1977). Pro-Japanese forces were especially large in Burma and Indonesia. These forces eventually took part in the subsequent struggle for independence after 1945. In Indonesia, the main military force the Japanese created was the Tentara Pembela Tanah Air (Peta, or "Army of the Defenders of the Homeland"). Another feature of the Japanese military imprint was the organization and training of numerous paramilitary groups, such as in Java. While the military training of these groups was minimal, the numbers of young men involved were considerable (Lebra 1977: 9). These forces, especially Peta, had a powerful influence on political leadership and on the Indonesian Army in postwar Indonesia.

Japan had already provided military training to a group of ethnic Burmans prior to the invasion of Burma in December 1941. Later renowned as

"The Thirty Comrades," this group of nationalists led by Aung San formed the core of the Bamar Lutlatye Tatmadaw (or "Burma Independence Army"), which entered Burma with the Japanese in early 1942. The Japanese recruited mostly Burmans but avoided ethnic minorities who had served in the colonial forces (Lebra 1977: 167). In mid-1942, the Japanese military command replaced the Bamar Lutlatye Tatmadaw with the considerably smaller, still ethnically Burman Burma Defense Army. When the Japanese proclaimed "independence" for Burma in late 1943, Aung San became Minister of Defense in the new Burmese government. In March 1945, he switched allegiances and led the Burma National Army (the renamed Burma Defense Army) out of Rangoon to join the Allied forces. In contrast, in Malaya, Sumatra, Borneo, and Timor-Leste, the Japanese nurtured smaller volunteer militaries, but they had no intent to foster or encourage nationalism or independence aspirations among the local populaces.

Unlike the case of the Dutch East Indies, where many Indonesians had initially welcomed the Japanese as liberators, Japan failed to win strong political support among local elites and populations in Malaya or in the Philippines. The traditional Malay elites, who the British had courted as a bulwark against communist agitation on the Peninsula, remained indifferent vis-à-vis the Japanese rhetoric of anticolonialism, whereas the Chinese population suffered disproportionally from Japanese repression. From February 1942 onward, the communist Malayan People's Anti-Japanese Army, mostly supported by the Chinese minority, organized the armed resistance on the Peninsula. Although the Japanese occupational authorities established a puppet government under President José Laurel in the Philippines, most of the Filipino elites were unwilling to collaborate with the occupiers, not least because the United States had already granted a transition to independence before the Japanese had attacked (Horner 1973). Instead, in Central Luzon, the peasant-based Hukbalahap, or "Huks," contributed an estimated 10,000 to 12,000 armed fighters to the anti-Japanese struggle (Ahmad 2009: 220). After the war, both the Communist Party of Malaya and the Huks continued the armed struggle against the returned British and the Philippine government.

In Indochina, Japan had allowed the French Vichy collaborationist administration to remain in place. However, in March 1945, Japanese forces disarmed and interned the French community and declared Vietnam independent, with Nguyen Emperor Bao Dai as nominal ruler. The intervention of an already weakened Japan enabled the Vietnam Independence League, known as Viet Minh, and the People's Liberation Armed Forces (renamed Vietnam People's Army in 1950) to fill the power vacuum (Thayer 2003). The Viet Minh under the leadership of Ho Chi Minh, alias Nguyen Ta Thanh, started a revolutionary insurgency and quickly gained full control over all of Vietnam. Ho Chi Minh proclaimed the Democratic Republic of Vietnam in Hanoi on September 2, 1945.

Unwilling to give up its colonial empire, France took control over the south but had to recognize the Democratic Republic of Vietnam as a sovereign state within the French Union. In December 1946, fighting broke out between colonial and communist troops. The First Indochina War lasted until French troops were decisively defeated in the battle of Dien Bien Phu in 1954. Negotiations between Paris and Hanoi, without participants from South Vietnam, resulted in the Geneva Accords. Under the Accords, Vietnam was to remain separated at the 17th parallel, the troops of both sides were to be withdrawn, and a supervisory commission would be put in place to oversee countrywide elections (Stockwell 1999: 43). Yet the elections never took place, and North and South Vietnam remained separated. While the North aligned with the Soviet Union and China, the South came under American influence.

2.3 Decolonization and State-Building

Within a remarkably short time, all Southeast Asian nations that achieved independence between 1946 (Philippines) and 1965 (Singapore) created military establishments, often based on the legacies of colonial armies, and merged colonial and anticolonial elements into facsimiles of Western armed services or, in the case of North Vietnam, a Soviet-style party-military (Table 2).

However, different backgrounds from which the members of the new officer corps came often created internal fissures. For example, in Indonesia, Japanese-trained members of Peta and irregular militia units and the former colonial army soldiers were uneasily joined in the Tentara Keamanan Rakyat ("People's Security Forces") in October 1945 (Hoadley 1975: 153), and politically mobilized factionalism – especially between former Peta officers and professionally trained officers – shaped intramilitary conflicts from the 1940s until the mid-1950s (Crouch 1978).

Following the Anglo-Burman Agreement in September 1945, units of the British colonial army dominated by Karen and Chin soldiers merged with former guerilla troops in one military organization, with ethnicity-based battalions. Because its founders and leaders were politicians first and foremost, the Bama Tatmadaw was at its inception a "political movement in military garb" (Guyot 1966). Unsurprisingly, by independence in 1948, the Tatmadaw had developed numerous factions based on ideological convictions, ethnic identities, personal loyalties, and allegiances to political parties (Callahan 2005: 112–13).

Table 2 Colonial Rule, Independence, and the Formation of Armed Forces

Country	Colonial power	Year of national independence	Method of achieving independence	Formation of national armed forces
Brunei	Great Britain	1984	Peaceful	1961
Burma/ Myanmar	Great Britain	1948	Peaceful	1941
Cambodia	France	1953	Peaceful	1946
Indonesia	Netherlands	1949	Revolutionary	1945
Laos	France	1953	Peaceful	1949
Malaysia	Great Britain	1957	Peaceful	1957
North Vietnam	France	1955	Revolutionary	1944
Philippines	Spain/USA	1946	Peaceful	1935
South Vietnam	France	1955	Revolutionary	1955
Siam/ Thailand	–	–	–	1852
Singapore	Great Britain	1965	Peaceful	1965
Timor-Leste	Portugal[a]	2002	Violent	2001

[a] In November 1975, the Timorese government unilaterally declared independence from Portugal. The following month, Indonesian troops occupied Timor-Leste.

In Cambodia, Laos, and Vietnam, the French after 1946 absorbed troops of colonial, guerrilla, and/or religious sect armies into a number of newly created regular armies. From the beginning, these forces were weakened by factionalism, personal favoritism, and political disputes. Postindependence leaders contributed to these fissures by nurturing personal loyalists at the expense of merit-based, "professionalized" promotions (Hoadley 1975: 69–76).

On the contrary, the armed forces in Malaysia, Singapore, and the Philippines were unified and homogeneous by Southeast Asian standards at that time. As mentioned previously, pro-Japanese militias were smaller in number, and the Japanese failed to win strong political support among indigenous political elites. Furthermore, Britain and the United States had established and integrated native troops into their colonial armies before World War II. These units then became the core of the postcolonial armies.

The Singapore Armed Forces were only formally established after Singapore's separation from Malaysia in August 1965. At that time, the local military and police forces were almost exclusively Malay, although Chinese people accounted for about three-fourths of the city's population. However, with the introduction of male conscription in 1967, for which Malays were not called up, the recruitment of Singaporean Malays stopped, and the Singaporean military became a Chinese-dominated service (Walsh 2007: 275).

In addition to legacies of colonial rule and Japanese occupation, the manner in which countries achieved independence and whether the political leaders of the new nations were challenged by armed insurgencies also strongly influenced the emerging types of civil–military relations. Where independence was achieved without significant bloodshed and civilian elites were able to build strong political parties and other institutions while simultaneously consolidating their political authority, the military's position vis-à-vis the civilian authorities was weaker. In contrast, revolutionary struggle, communal insurgencies, and weak political institutions reinforced the preponderance of military elites relative to civilians. Where the military played a prominent role in the processes of decolonization and suppressing communal unrest, Asian militaries subsequently mythologized their role as creator-guardians of the state and "nation."

In contrast to the Western experience, warfare in most of Southeast Asia was not directed against "external" enemies but instead against enemies that could be identified as "internal" (Callahan 2005: 9; cf. Table 3). Consequently, the military's main mission was internal security. With the exception of the socialist armies of Vietnam and Laos, no military in the region has been in major interstate warfare after 1946. Despite occasional border skirmishes between states, intrastate wars are the prevalent form of armed conflict in Southeast Asia. In fact, other than Brunei and Singapore, all Southeast Asian armies have significant experience in fighting civil wars or armed insurrections.

In Burma, the "Burmanization of Tatmadaw" (Selth 2002: 264) was a direct result of the outbreak of several rebellions against the central government almost immediately after independence in January 1948.[4] Following the breakaway of pro-communist factions and several ethnic minority units, the army was down to barely 2,000 troops when General Ne Win took command of the Tatmadaw in February 1949 (Callahan 2005: 114–15). Ne Win quickly reorganized the army under a centralized command, expanded troop strength, and modernized its equipment. This allowed the government to regain control over most of the Union's territories (Selth 2002:10–11; Callahan 2005: 17). With the successful counterinsurgency operations of the early 1950s and the "cleansing" of the non–Ne Win factions during the first military government (1958–60), the

---

[4] However, scholars have emphasized the fact that despite the dominance of Bamar senior officers at the highest levels of the Tatmadaw, racial background has been less of an issue in promotions than social and religious backgrounds. Officers from ethnic minority groups (i.e., Shan, Mon, or Rakhine) can reach the ranks of colonel or above as long as they are Buddhist.

Table 3 Liberation Wars, Class-Based and Communal Insurgencies, and
International Wars, 1946–76

Country	Extrastate (liberation) wars	Intrastate wars		Interstate wars
		Class based	Communal	
Brunei	–	–	–	–
Burma	No	Yes	Yes	No
Cambodia	No	Yes	No	No
Timor-Leste	Yes	Yes[a]	No	No
Indonesia	Yes	Yes	Yes	No
Laos	No	Yes	Yes	Yes[b]
Malaysia	No	Yes[c]		No
Philippines	No	Yes	Yes	No
Singapore	No	No	No	No
Thailand	No	Yes	No[d]	No
Vietnam[e]	Yes	Yes	No	Yes

Note: Wars as defined by the Correlates of War (COW) project (1,000 battle-related fatalities or more per year). Wars often contain elements of different types of wars and can, over their life span, transform, for instance, from nonstate into extrastate war (i.e., Timor-Leste in 1975–76). Civil wars yet can include interventions by other states (i.e., Cambodia in 1970–71).

[a] War of 1975 between Fretilin and other Timor-Lesteese groups, followed by war between Indonesian troops and Fretilin (1975–79).
[b] US-led "secret war" (1968–73).
[c] The communist insurgency of 1946–57 was mainly supported by members of the Chinese minority; hence class-based and ethnic tensions reinforced each other.
[d] The Malay–Muslim insurgency (1960–77) is categorized as a low-intensity conflict.
[e] North and South Vietnam.

Source: Sarkees and Whelon Wayman 2010.

Tatmadaw became a remarkably unified military organization (Selth 2002: 259).

In Indonesia, the military struggle against the Dutch, who had reoccupied the archipelago in 1945, and campaigns against insurgencies in the South Moluccas (1950) and the regional Darul Islam rebellion (1953) had a profound impact on the armed forces, renamed in 1947 to Tentara Nasional Indonesia (TNI). During the independence struggle from 1945 to 1949, the army developed the strategy of "total defense" and divided its force between a mobile guerrilla wing that attacked Dutch forces and the territorial army, deployed to specific locations to organize local communities to resist. This mixture of guerilla warfare and territorial management became the blueprint for the Indonesian army's "territorial command system" that paralleled the civilian government structure and entrenched military structures in Indonesian society (Crouch 1978). The "total defense" strategy and the territorial structure developed in the 1940s remain essentially in place at present.

The pivotal role of the military during the liberation war and in quelling various rebellions and dissident movements after 1949 provided the foundation for the military's concept of a "middle way," according to which the TNI would neither submit to civilian supremacy nor assume full control of government. This was later transformed into the *dwifungsi* ("dual function") doctrine. According to this doctrine, the TNI had a special function in defining and preserving the Indonesian state, and its mission therefore included two equally important functions: a military function and a sociopolitical function (Alagappa 1988: 24–25). Within a decade of independence, military personnel became heavily engaged in political decision making and commercial activities and established themselves as relatively autonomous power centers to which governments were beholden.

In contrast, the armed forces of Malaysia and the Philippines emerged out of relatively orderly colonial handover of political power to local elites rather than through revolutionary conflict. Even though Malaya confronted a communist uprising from 1946 to 1957, the main responsibility for counterinsurgency was borne by troops of the Commonwealth and the Malay police, both under British command (Nathan and Govindasamy 2001: 262).

As in Malaysia, the military in the Philippines had no role in the process of decolonization, depriving it of a strong source of legitimacy. However, different Filipino administrations deployed the military as an indispensable apparatus to uphold order and security in the countryside, a marked contrast with Malaysia and Singapore. From 1950 to 1954, the AFP fought the Huk rebels, which expanded the nontraditional roles of the military, including organizing development projects, working law enforcement and local administration, assisting the national election commission, and serving in cabinet posts (Kessler 1989: 218–19). From 1968 onward, the army engaged a renewed communist guerrilla resistance, and since the early 1970s, it fought Muslim insurgents in Mindanao. Over time, the focus on internal security and civic assistance perforated most of the border between military and civilian spheres of competencies (Hall 2017).

2.4 Militaries and Regime Formation

Historical and structural contexts are important, but they alone cannot explain why military rule prevailed in Indonesia, South Vietnam, and Burma but not in

Malaysia, North Vietnam, and the Philippines. Rather, civilian elite cohesion and party politics were other important causal factors. Consensually unified civilian elites and strong party institutions generated conditions that minimized both the incentives for politicians to pull the military into the domain of government and the opportunity for military leaders to push into civilian politics (Slater 2010b). In contrast, weak institutionalization of civilian political organizations and the lack of sustained support for political structures led civilian political groups to rely heavily on the military's coercive and organizational powers to establish state structures and enforce the political elites' claim to power. This empowered militaries vis-à-vis the civilian elites and ultimately led to the emergence of praetorian militaries.

An illuminating example is the Burmese Tatmadaw, which had grown into a "state within a state" and an economic powerhouse by the mid-1950s. Military officers exercised wide administrative and political power while conducting counterinsurgency operations and, with the army's "defense service industry," dominated shipping, banking, imports-exports, hotels, and tourism (Yawnghwe 1997: 90–91). Notably, improvements in civilian political or bureaucratic structures did not keep pace with the transformation of the army state organizations. One party – the Anti-Fascist People's Freedom League (AFPFL) – had been at the forefront of Burmese politics after 1945. Founded as a merger of the Burma National Army led by Aung San, the Communist Party of Burma, and the People's Revolutionary Party in March 1945, the AFPFL managed to win the elections of 1947, 1951, and 1956. The party enjoyed a monopoly on power that reflected its strong support especially among Bamar voters, but it suffered from factionalism (Taylor 1996). Factional conflicts within the AFPFL forced Premier U Nu to appoint a caretaker military government in 1958. The government of General Ne Win from 1958 to 1960 convinced many in the military leadership that they could do a better job of running the country than the civilian politicians (Selth 2002: 12). Before the 1960 election, the party broke into two factions, the military-backed Stable AFPFL and U Nu's Clean AFPFL (Steinberg 2010). The military handed back control to an elected government, but U Nu's decision to declare Buddhism the state religion triggered a new wave of ethnic rebellions. Finally, General Ne Win staged a coup d'état in 1962. For the following 50 years, the military in one form or another ruled the country.

In Indonesia, the anticolonial struggle had left the new nation with a wide array of political forces, including secular nationalists, communists, traditionalist and modernist Islamic parties, and the military. Following a series of short-lived parliamentary governments, Indonesia's founder-president Sukarno established his authoritarian "Guided Democracy" based on the doctrines of corporatist "functional groups" (*golongan karya*, Golkar) and *Pancasila* in 1957 (Feith 1962). Despite the army's hostility, Sukarno strengthened his ties with the communists and followed an increasingly erratic economic and foreign policy (Sundhausen 1982: 156). In 1965, the social, political, and economic structures of the new nation were near collapse (Ricklefs 2008: 338). On the night of September 30, 1965, a group of left-leaning air force officers killed several members of the military leadership in a botched coup attempt. In retaliation, the military under General Suharto, along with anticommunist groups, orchestrated a violent campaign against real or suspected communists that killed half a million citizens in 1965 and 1966. Once the communist movement was destroyed, Suharto took over executive control from Sukarno and, in 1968, the presidency as well.

As in other regions when socialist movements engaged in revolutionary struggle against colonial or anticommunist regimes, liberation armies in Indochina fought a Maoist "People's War" under the guidance of a Communist Party. The "People's Army" was an instrument of the worker-peasant alliance led by the Party against the capitalist class and Western imperialism. However, guerilla war as a form of politicomilitary combat assigned an important role in propaganda and political work, internal security, economic production, and social development to the military, which inevitably led to the fusion of political and military elites (Vasavakul 2001: 341–47).

While "political generals" led communist armies until well after national reunification in North Vietnam and Laos (Turley 1977: 233), the South Vietnamese defense forces were mainly a creature of French colonial policy. President Diem (1955–63) moved to consolidate his authority over the military by building a network of army officers whose loyalty to him was based on their common Catholic or central Vietnamese (the president's home region) ties, recent promotion, or outright payoff in cash (Hoadley 1975: 72–85). However, a military coup led to the assassination of Diem in November 1963, which was followed by a series of unstable military-dominated governments until the South Vietnamese state collapsed in April 1975. Similarly, the Royal Lao Armed Forces were constantly weakened by military factionalism based on personal disputes and kinship competition (Lipp and Chambers 2017: 221). There were coup attempts in 1960, 1964, 1965, 1966, and 1973, and the military soon degenerated into a decentralized group of warlords and military cliques who were more concerned with promoting their economic interests than fighting the Pathet Lao, the military branch of the Lao Communist Party (Hoadley 1975).

For the first 15 years or so after independence, it seemed that Cambodia would develop differently than the rest of Indochina. During the personalist

rule of King Norodom Sihanouk (1955–70), the military's activities emphasized civic action, rural development, and sporadic counterguerrilla operations
against Cambodian communists (the so-called Khmer Rouge), but soldiers
were minimally involved in national politics (Hoadley 1975: 134). However,
in October 1970, anticommunist and anti-Vietnamese politicians and military
officers organized a coup d'état against Sihanouk. Marshall Lon Nol, a former
minister of defense and prime minister, became president of the newly proclaimed republic. His regime was "dominated by army generals and colonels,
and supported by an American military aid mission" (Hoadley 1975: 128).
Following the fall of Phnom Penh in April 1975 and the Khmer Rouge's four-
year reign of terror, Vietnamese troops invaded Cambodia in December 1978.
The pro-Vietnamese government of the People's Republic of Kampuchea
(from 1989 on, State of Cambodia) created its own military. Following the
Vietnamese model and with military assistance from Hanoi, the Cambodian
People's Armed Forces main task was to support the Vietnamese occupation
forces in countering the guerilla war waged by the so-called Coalition
Government of Democratic Kampuchea.[5] While superficially similar to the
revolutionary party-militaries in Vietnam and Laos, the communist military
in Cambodia lacked the effectiveness and ideological commitment that characterized the Vietnamese army and the degree of cohesion and discipline of
the dual party-military elite in Laos. Under the United Nations interim
administration from 1991 to 1993, the official armed forces were merged
with the royalist and former pro–Lon Nol guerrilla units. This created a
factionalized and oversized military shaped by personal loyalties and patrimonial relations (see Section 3).

Malaysia presents a contrasting case to these instances of military praetorianism. When Malaysia gained independence in 1957, British officers still held
most top command posts of the Malaysian defense force, and the joint Anglo-
Malayan Defense Agreement preserved Britain's right and obligation to defend
Malaya and station forces on the Peninsula. The British military presence
and the defeat of the communist insurgency prior to full national sovereignty
meant that Malaysia's political leaders could give priority to socioeconomic
development rather than to building a large military, making the military "a
latecomer in Malaysian institutional development" (Ahmed 1988: 235). It was
only after the British withdrawal in 1971 that the government began to invest in
a military buildup in earnest (Beeson and Bellamy 2008: 86). By then, well-
institutionalized communal parties had already monopolized access to political

---

[5] A coalition of the Khmer Rouge, royalists, and former pro-Lon Nol-forces, formally led by
Norodom Sihanouk.

power under the umbrella of a multiethnic coalition of political parties, initially known as the "Alliance" and since 1973 as *Barisan Nasional* ("National Front"; Slater 2010b: 154). The "elite protection pact" (Slater 2010b: 154) between Malay, Chinese, and Indian elites (known as the "Bargain") resulted in a political and economic order that protected the interests of both the elites and their ethnic constituencies. Following communal riots in 1969, the Alliance/ *Barisan Nasional* was able to recalibrate the political order in a more authoritarian form, but avoiding military intrusion into politics (Crouch 1996). However, it is important to recognize that the system of civil–military relations based on the formal separation of civilian and military authorities was always contingent on the continuation of Malay dominance of the political system that has prevailed for decades (Nathan and Govindasamy 2001).

Resembling the experience of the revolutionary party regime in North Vietnam, the Singaporean Defense Force was created by the People's Action Party (PAP), which has been in power since 1959. The PAP, led by Prime Minister Lee Kuan Yew, had its own vision of a Singaporean military, inspired and influenced by the Israeli model of a conscript army, and the subordination of the military to government in a system of civil–military relations that lacks the strict separation between government/political elite and the military elite (Huxley 2000; see Section 3).

As mentioned previously, almost immediately after the Philippines achieved its independence in 1946, the AFP focused on internal security and socio-economic development. Yet it was not until the government of President Marcos (1965–86) that the principle of civilian supremacy as the centerpiece of Philippine civil–military relations began to erode. Before the ascendance of President Ferdinand Marcos and despite weakly institutionalized political parties, a cohesive civilian elite – well entrenched in the state and the economy and dominating Filipino politics at all levels – had accepted elections as the only legitimate route to political office (Landé 1965). Since commissions and promotions were based on civilian patronage, military officers depended on the support of president, Congress, and local politicians. This precluded the development not only of an officer corps with values distinct from the civilian population in terms of ruling ambitions but also the thorough professionalization of the AFP (Hernandez 1985). With the support of senior military officers, Ferdinand Marcos, who was elected president in 1965 and reelected in 1969, declared martial law in 1972. Following his self-coup that allowed him to preside for another 14 years over an increasingly despotic regime, Marcos perfected his patrimonial control of the AFP to such an extent that in the early 1980s it "looked more like Marcos's Praetorian Guard than a properly professional military" (Hedman 2001: 178).

Thailand's soldiers could not claim "freedom fighter" status as in Burma and Indonesia. Nonetheless, the military played a key role in the post-1932 authoritarian order. Under the bureaucratic polity, competition over political and economic influence led to factional struggles within the military (Tamada 1995: 320). The balance of power between informal yet close-knit cliques shifted considerably over time. This resulted in frequent changes in the military leadership, and the coup d'état became a common way to seize power, because the country experienced at least 14 coup attempts between 1933 and 1991 (Thanet 2001). Especially after the 1947 coup, the military became increasingly involved in Thailand's economy, and an impenetrable complex of military-run businesses inside and outside of the state soon emerged (Chambers and Waitoolkiat 2017: 43).

3 Types of Civil–Military Relations

Employing the analytical framework introduced in Section 1, the different forms of civil–military relations in the region since the 1950s can be organized into four groups (Table 4). As reflected in Table 4, civil–military relations in some Southeast Asian countries have undergone substantial changes over the last six decades, but there have been significant continuities as well. Most important, in almost all countries that experienced democratic changes since the late 1980s, the new political environment necessitated reforms of civil–military relations because the old authoritarian patterns and modes of civil–military interaction were no longer sustainable. In postauthoritarian Philippines and Indonesia (but not in Thailand), democratic reforms in civil–military relations and the broader polity have contributed to more professional civil–military relations, although they still exhibit praetorian features and, hence, are classified as hybrid types.

3.1 Praetorian Civil–Military Relations

Burma/Myanmar, Thailand, South Vietnam, and presocialist Laos, as well as Indonesia until 1998, build the group of countries with praetorian civil–military relations, or military dominance over the political system, characterized by a high frequency of military coups and extended periods of direct military rule (or both). Following the 1962 coup d'état that brought General Ne Win to power, the Tatmadaw came to dominate almost every aspect of Burmese society, economy, and politics. From 1962 to 1974, the generals governed via a Ruling Council and then through the Burma Socialist Program Party (BSPP). Unlike Indonesia's Golkar Party, in which civilian bureaucrats and politicians had a voice, the BSPP was entirely controlled by military officers, beholden, in

Table 4 Types of Political–Military Relations in Southeast Asia, 1950–2015

Country	1950	1970	1980	2015
Brunei	–	–	–	Professional
Cambodia	–	Neopatrimonial	Revolutionary	Neopatrimonial
Indonesia	Praetorian	Praetorian	Praetorian	Praetorian/professional
Laos	–	Praetorian	Revolutionary	Revolutionary
Malaysia	–	Professional	Professional	Professional
Myanmar	Praetorian	Praetorian	Praetorian	Praetorian
Philippines	Professional	Professional	Neopatrimonial	Praetorian/professional
Singapore	–	Professional	Professional	Professional
Thailand	Praetorian	Praetorian	Praetorian	Praetorian
Timor-Leste	–	–	–	Neopatrimonial
(North) Vietnam	Revolutionary	Revolutionary	Revolutionary	Revolutionary
South Vietnam	–	Praetorian	–	–

Source: The author.

turn, to their military superiors, while civilian state agencies became "medieval fiefdoms" that "responded less and less to rational-legal norms, and increasingly to the 'logic' of opaque, patrimonial military politics and intrigues" (Yawnghwe 1997: 96–97).

Spiraling inflation, a fuel and rice shortage, and the complete demonetization of small banknotes in September 1987 triggered a popular uprising in 1988. Protests reached an initial peak on August 8 ("8–8–88 Uprising"), and despite a brutal crackdown in which about 3,000 people were killed, the country was swept by another wave of mass protests in September 1988 (Ferrara 2003). Finally, on September 18, the Tatmadaw's chief of staff, General Saw Maung, installed the State Law and Order Restoration Council (SLORC). Army troops began a four-day-long massacre with several thousands of civilian casualties. Under heavy restrictions, elections took place in 1990, but the military nullified the results when the National League for Democracy, led by Aung San Suu Kyi, achieved a landslide victory. Instead, the SLORC (since 1997, State Peace and Development Council [SPDC]) reinforced direct military rule.

After 1990, the short-term goal of the military government was to ensure its own survival in power, whereas its longer-term goal was "to put into place all necessary means to guarantee that the Tatmadaw would remain the real arbiter of power in Myanmar" after a handover of government to the civilians (Selth 2002: 33). For that purpose, the Tatmadaw first contained more immediate threats from insurgents and dissident groups. Ceasefire agreements with around thirty rebel groups and the failure of protests by Buddhist monks in 2007 ("Saffron Revolution") signaled the extent to which the military had managed to realize this aim. This enabled the regime to introduce a new political structure that relieved the Tatmadaw of its administrative burden while disguising the armed forces' continued control of the country's more important political processes.

In 2008, the SPDC presented a new constitution that granted the Tatmadaw immense political prerogatives and veto powers. The sham elections in November 2010 and the formation of a government under President Thein Sein, a former general, in 2011 completed the transition from direct military rule to multiparty authoritarianism under military tutelage. Since then, several political reforms followed, including a national dialogue with opposition leader Aung San Suu Kyi and the 2015 general elections, in which the opposition won a majority of seats in the bicameral Union legislature.

Nonetheless, the Tatmadaw remains the country's most powerful political actor. For example, it has a 25 percent representation in the Union legislature as well as in the regional parliaments, which guarantees the military a veto over any prospects of constitutional change. It controls the Ministries of Home

Affairs, Defense, and Border Areas and maintains a majority representation in the National Defense and Security Council. It enjoys complete autonomy in its internal affairs, and the constitution provides the military with the legitimate right to act independently to ensure compliance with the constitution (Croissant and Lorenz 2018: 185–89, 200–2). Most important, internal security operations of the Tatmadaw such as attacks against Rohingya Muslims in the Northern Rakhine State in 2017–18 remain beyond the control of the civilian government. As Renaud Egreteau (2017: 125) aptly concludes, the "provisions of the 2008 constitution are essentially extending – and legalizing – the prerogatives, political interventionism, and legal immunity of the Burmese army in a very praetorian – yet constitutionally legal – way."

The extraordinary durability of military rule from 1962 to 2010 and the success of the Tatmadaw in controlling a top-down transition from military rule to military tutelage are due to a confluence of a number of factors. First, the military government of 1962 and the SLORC/SPDC government were the result of military interventions supported by key military elites, included all major intramilitary power groups, and led to the institutionalization of a military regime hierarchically led by senior military officers.

Second, military governments managed to institutionalize power-sharing arrangements between different groups of military elites, which made sure that no individual faction would be able to undermine the power base of the military-in-government within the military-as-institution (Croissant and Kamerling 2013). Even though the Tatmadaw suffered from factional conflicts, these were always defused, or the renegade factions were purged before they could threaten regime survival (Win Min 2008: 1018–37).

Third, in order to improve the morale of its officers and soldiers and to consolidate its grip over the country and the military-as-institution, the SLORC/SPDC junta undertook massive efforts to modernize and enlarge the Tatmadaw and established new military–administrative institutions (Selth 2002; Myoe 2007). The SPDC government after 1997 strengthened the authority of the commander-in-chief, enhanced the position of the Ministry of Defense, and placed elite combat units under the control of the Bureau for Special Operations (Callahan 2005: 211). Prior to 2004, the government also relied on the Directorate of Defense Services Intelligence to monitor military units (Fink 2009: 168–70), but conflicts between military intelligence and other military services led to a purge of senior intelligence officers and the installation of a new intelligence service, the Military Affairs Security (Win Min 2008: 1028–30). Finally, the post-1988 junta strengthened direct military control over the most lucrative branches of the national economy, offered military families and veterans privileged access to public services, and allowed regional commanders and military units to pursue their own commercial interests (Steinberg 2010: 101; see Section 4).

Similar to Burma, the New Order regime of President Suharto (1967–98) was originally a military regime, and the military was the predominant political force within the government, second only to the president himself (Slater 2010b). This was reflected in the further entrenchment of the territorial structure that "facilitated the New Order's grip on the provinces, as Suharto also used the territorial system to ensure the army could exert direct pressure on rural voters" (Raymond 2017: 162). Furthermore, under the *dwifungsi* doctrine, the military became entwined with political institutions, most evident in its dominant position in the regime's main sociopolitical organization, Golkar (which had been founded by a group of army officers in 1964), its reserved seats in national and subnational parliaments, and the occupation of many civilian administrative positions, minister posts, and governorships by active soldiers.[6] In addition, the Indonesian military expanded and deepened its economic and commercial roles, leading observers to consider this the third role in an expanded *trifungsi* (McCulloch 2003).

In contrast to Myanmar, however, Indonesia's so-called New Order experienced a double transformation of personalization and substantial "civilianization," limiting the autonomous role of the military but also creating to some extent a separation between armed forces and the regime. Because the dictator feared that "an expanding army might turn against him" (Mietzner 2017: 3), he reduced the size of the armed forces from 346,000 troops in 1967 to 250,000 in 1981 and 280,000 in 1997, the last full year of his presidency. Suharto also cut the defense budget – in relative terms – from 42.7 percent of central government expenditure (CGE) to 12.1 and 7.1 percent over the same period (Bureau of Arms Control, Verification, and Compliance 2017).

When Suharto began civilianizing Golkar in the early 1980s, the military was no longer able to influence politics without Suharto's backing (Tomsa 2008: 39). Consequently, "what started as a system of oligarchic military rule evolved into a highly personalized regime, backed in nearly equal measure by military and civilian organizations" (Slater 2010a: 133). Meanwhile, Suharto could rely on the army to control and, if necessary, repress political parties, civil society, and media (Aspinall 2005).

Suharto's misuse of the military promotion system and patronage politics generated internal divisions, and by the mid-1990s, the military was factionalized into "losers" and "winners" of Suharto's "franchise system" (McLeod

---

[6] In 1981, at the height of its *dwifungsi* privileges, its officers held 8,025 civil positions, including 28 of 63 ambassadorial posts, 14 of 19 secretary-generalships of ministries, and 18 of 27 governorships (Said 2006).

2008: 200). While the status of the military as part of the New Order coalition experienced a significant decline over time, this also created to some extent a separation between the military-as-institution and the regime. Moreover, the demise of Suharto's regime as a consequence of mass protests during the Asian financial crisis in May 1998 did not significantly undermine the institutional capacity of the armed services (Mietzner 2009).

The democratization reform process (*reformasi*) of the late 1990s and early 2000s led to significant changes in the political roles of the TNI. The military and the police were formally separated, and when the military gave up its *dwifungsi* doctrine, active officers had to leave most posts in the civilian administration. The military cut its ties with Golkar, lost its reserved seats in national and subnational legislatures, and had to allow its "foundations" (*yayasan*), which managed some of its property and investments, to be audited (Croissant et al. 2013).

Despite these reforms, the legacies of the (pre-)New Order era have not been fully overcome. For example, the TNI still maintains unaccountable commercial activities and has successfully blocked any political attempt to abolish the army's territorial structure and to redirect its role to external defense. Instead, the so-called war on terrorism has created an institutional opportunity to regain lost ground in internal security operations, where the TNI has again become the dominant actor (Honna 2017: 315–16). Furthermore, the military still strongly influences the Ministry of Defense, and parliament lacks the capability to oversee defense affairs (Gunawan 2017). Moreover, as former military officers (or *purnawirawan*) play an increasingly important role in electoral and party politics, military officers have again gained access to patronage politics in both parliament and political parties (Aminuddin 2017). Beginning with the 2004 presidential contest, some former military officers have created their own political parties, and many *purnawirwan* began to play a crucial role in the campaign teams of other, ostensibly civilian-dominated political parties (Aminuddin 2017). Even though since 1999 officers must retire from active service before standing for office and the power of *purnawirawan* is limited to individuals, this development provides new opportunities for the military to maintain its economic and political interests. Finally, as Marcus Mietzner (2018: 140–41) notes, the TNI continues "to yield considerable political power" in postauthoritarian Indonesia because elected presidents such as Susilo Bambang Yudhoyono and Joko Widodo viewed the armed forces as a key part of their presidential coalitions in order to counterbalance against possible civilian defections. In return for the political loyalty of military leaders, these civilian leaders have refrained from tackling deeper reforms in the defense sector.

Thailand is the third Southeast Asian country with a strong praetorian tradition. Under the bureaucratic polity, civilian bureaucrats and military elites dominated Thai politics, while King Bhumibol Adulyadej (Rama IX, r. 1946–2016) lent legitimacy to the military–bureaucratic elites. Although the military–bureaucratic elites formed the only organized political group in society from 1932 until the 1970s, "they were not united" (Samudavanija 1989: 320). Furthermore, long-term processes of economic and social change and the rise of private business and political parties starting in the late 1950s weakened the power of the bureaucratic forces. With the rise of provincial business elites and political parties, the disunity that had existed between elites increased, while, at the same time, fissures between old and new elites began to emerge (Case 2002). In the 1980s, an electoral authoritarian regime emerged with a popularly elected lower house, an appointed Senate (whose members were primarily recruited from the state bureaucracy and the military), and a retired military officer as unelected prime minister. Simultaneously, the palace regained political influence and power by forging "a modern form of monarchy as a para-political institution," which Duncan McCargo described as the "network monarchy." At its heart, the power of the network monarchy "relied on placing the right people . . . in the right jobs" (McCargo 2005: 501), including a network of loyalist officers inside the "monarchised military" (Chambers and Waitoolkiat 2016), which enabled the palace to intervene actively in political developments even after Thailand launched a transition to democracy in May 1992 (McCargo 2005: 508).

While the Thai armed forces "seemed prepared to maintain a low-key political presence" (Funston 2006: 348), after 1992, democratization and civilian control were to be realized only to the extent that they did not threaten the position of the "network monarchy" or the ideas that under-pinned its power (Hewison and Kengkij 2010: 180). This became obvious during the premiership of Thaksin Shinawatra (2001–6), who attempted to sever the relationship between the monarchy and the military and to turn the latter into a tool of his personal rule. However, this ultimately brought the confrontation between the military leadership and Thaksin to a head and, as an unintended consequence, culminated in the 2006 coup d'état (Pathmanand 2008).

Even though the military allowed free parliamentary elections in December 2007 and handed power back to an elected pro-Thaksin government, military leaders continued to intervene whenever they deemed necessary for their own benefit or to defend the monarchy. Most important, on May 22, 2014, the army, led by Army Chief Prayuth Chan-ocha, staged a coup d'état against Prime Minister Yingluck Shinawatra, Thaksin's sister.

The 2006 and 2014 coups were staged by military officers claiming deep loyalty to the monarchy. Yet the two putsches differ from previous coups as well as from each other. The first difference is that the political role of the military since the 1940s had been justified in terms of the defense of national institutions and later – as in February 1991 – stressed rampant government corruption, the emergence of deep divisions in society, and attacks on the military (Tamada 1995). In 2006, however, the coup leaders justified their actions as a means to "restore democracy," whereas in 2014 the narrative of returning the country to order and defending the monarchy was dominant (Pathmanand 2008; Chambers and Waitoolkiat 2016).[7]

Second, as Eugénie Mérieau (2017: 140) asserts, military coup leaders "seem to have always favored the adoption of constitutions . . . as a common way to . . . consolidate power. Once in power, the new power-holders seek to entrench their preferences and interests in a new constitution." Interim constitutions focused on the ex-post legitimization of the coup and the coup group's actions, whereas constitutions that were intended to be more permanent focused mainly on preserving their political legacy and protecting coup leader's interests after leaving power (Mérieau 2017: 152). Since 1977, postcoup constitution-making was followed by elections that marked the return to "civilian" rule (see Table 5).

However, since the 2014 coup, the National Council for Peace and Order (NCPO) has pledged to hold a general election, but the generals have repeatedly delayed the poll. Moreover, the military maintained a tight grip on power, unlike in 1991 and 2006, when it quickly transferred most power to the cabinet, and General Prayuth himself simultaneously serves as NCPO chief and prime minister (Prasirtsuk 2015: 204–5). This reflects a lesson that the NCPO has drawn from the failure of the previous military government to neutralize the pro-Thaksin movement before organizing general elections. These actions and the strong military prerogatives in the 2017 constitution suggest that the generals want to preserve their role as guardian of the monarchy, state, and nation after the return to elections and (quasi-)civilian cabinets.

3.2 Revolutionary Civil–Military Relations

Revolutionary civil–military relations in socialist Vietnam and Laos, like all the fundamental dynamics of their political system, derive from the structural relationship between the Communist Party and the other institutions of the

---

[7] Additional factors likely strengthened the military's disposition for political intervention, such as approaching military reshuffles, the desire to ensure an orderly royal succession, and competition among military factions (Sirivunnabood and Ricks 2016: 10).

Table 5 Coups, Constitutions and Elections in Thailand, 1932–2017

Coup[a]	Constitution	Election[b]
June 1932	June 1932 (interim)	November 1933
	October 1932	
October 1933		
November 1947	November 1947	January 1948
October 1948		June 1949
February 1949	March 1949	
November 1951		February 1952
September 1957		December 1957
October 1958	January 1959	
October 1976	October 1976	
October 1977	November 1977 (interim)	April 1979
	December 1978	
February 1991	March 1991 (interim)	March 1992
	December 1991	
September2006	October 2006 (interim)	December 2007
	August 2006	
May 2014	May 2014 (interim)	
	April 2017	

[a] Between 1912 and 2017 there have been 20 coup attempts as well as 20 different constitutions in Thailand. This table shows only successful military coup d'états.
[b] Only elections for the House of Representatives.
Source: The author, based on Croissant and Lorenz 2018.

polity. The control over the political system rests securely with Party leaders, and political–military relations, though not free of frictions, remain stable. Although the Party directs and supervises all other institutions, there is no clear division between civilian Party elites and military elites. Furthermore, as in all communist systems, the military's subordination to the political leadership is ensured not by making the military a politically neutral tool but also by turning the army into a "party in uniform" (Perlmutter and LeoGrande 1982). While military leaders in Myanmar and Indonesia established political parties as vehicles for their hold on power, in Vietnam and Laos, the Party created the People's Army as a tool for enforcing its claim to power and realizing its ideological and political goals.

In contrast to most of postwar Eastern Europe, communist parties in Indochina came to power by successfully waging guerrilla war, a form of politicomilitary combat that inevitably led to the fusion of political and military elites and assigned an important role in the construction of a socialist society to the army (Vasavakul 2001; Dwyer 2014). Revolutionary parties in Laos and Vietnam enjoyed strong internal cohesion due to a common ideology that combined utopian social goals with strong nationalist ideals and through well-developed and hierarchical structures that channeled elite conflicts and mass mobilization. Just as the Soviet "Leninist" party was the standard for creating the revolutionary regime party, revolutionary party leaders in Indochina drew on the Soviet model to establish their party-armies and create mechanisms to ensure the military's loyalty.

Organizationally, military subordination in Vietnam is maintained by a chain of command that is composed of Party committees organized vertically from the Political Bureau and the Central Military Party Commission down through the company level of the armed forces. In Laos, the Central National Defense and Security Committee of the Politburo of the Communist Party also oversees the General Political Department of the Army. Additional Committees for National Defense and Security at the provincial level are led by the secretaries of local Party committees and are appointed by the Politburo. Also typical for revolutionary party-military relations is the Soviet model of a dual leadership of military offices and political commissars. Originally, both the Lao and Vietnam Communist Parties established this model of a dual chain of military and political command throughout the armed forces by appointing a political "deputy" commander for each military commander. These political commanders exercised official and unofficial control functions over their military command counterparts and also served to further Party interests by indoctrinating soldiers in Marxism-Leninism. This system was replaced in Vietnam (1979) and Laos (1985) by a one-commander system, which placed the ultimate authority and ideological responsibility in the hands of commanding military officers, although it was reintroduced in Vietnam in 1985 (Vasavakul 2001: 342–43; Stuart-Fox 2002: 310).

The party–army symbiosis during the period of guerrilla warfare was characterized by low levels of differentiation between military and nonmilitary elites and the circulation of elites between military and nonmilitary posts. Senior military officers served on the Politburo and the Central Committee of the Communist Party, while the armed forces, like other functional groups, enjoyed representation in the legislature and at the Party Congress. However, once the Communist Parties succeeded in establishing themselves in power and consolidated their rule, institutional boundaries began to solidify, and elite circulation between military and nonmilitary posts became more difficult. In fact, while virtually all the ingredients of Party control and the socialist Party-state are still in place, the most important changes in Party–military relations in recent decades concern the representation of the armed forces in

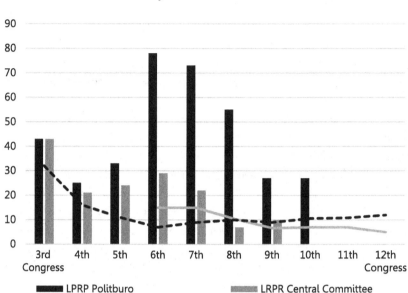

Figure 1 Proportion of military officers in the Central Committee and
Politburo of the Communist Parties in Laos and Vietnam

Note: Lao Party Congresses: 3rd in 1982, 4th in 1986, 5th in 1991, 6th in 1996, 7th in
2001, 8th in 2006, 9th in 2011, 10th in 2016. Vietnamese Party Congresses:3rd in 1960,
4th in 1976, 5th in 1982, 6th in 1986, 7th in 1991, 8th in 1996, 9th in 2001, 10th in 2006,
11th in 2011, 12th in 2016.

Source: Croissant and Lorenz 2018.

central Party organs (see Figure 1) as well as their economic role (see
Section 4).

As shown in Figure 1, the percentage of military members on the Central
Committee of the Vietnam Communist Party decreased from 31.9 percent at the
Third Party Congress (1960) to 12.1 percent at the Twelfth Party Congress
(2016). Simultaneously, the proportion of members appointed to the Politburo
from military ranks went from 15.4 to 5.2 percent. At the Twelfth Party
Congress, the police gained greater representation in the Politburo at the expense
of the military for the first time (Abuza and Nguyen Nhat Anh 2016). Originally,
the proportion of military men in the party's top decision-making bodies in Laos
was substantially larger than in Vietnam. The Sixth Party Congress (1996) had
an especially militarized Central Committee and Politburo, with 78 percent of
the Politburo and 29 percent of the Central Committee being active or retired
politicomilitary officers. At the height of military representation in Party and
state organs, the state president and general secretary of the Central Committee

of the Party, the chairman of the National Assembly, the prime minister, and up to six government ministers were active or former military officers (Stuart-Fox 2002: 243). However, the professionalization of Party organization and changes among leadership generations caused a sharp decline in the representation of military men in the Party's main bodies since 2001.

3.3 Professional Civil–Military Relations

Civilian primacy is a hallmark of political–military relations in Party-led autocracies such as Malaysia and Singapore but also Brunei, the only royal autocracy in the region. It was also a guiding principle of civil–military relations in the first Philippine democracy before 1972.

In all four cases, local troops of the colonial armies formed the nucleus of the new armed forces, which did not need to include anticolonial or pro-Japanese troops (see Section 2). Furthermore, governments retained strong military and defense ties with the former colonial powers. This included British troops stationed in Malaysia and Singapore (until 1971) and US guarantees for the external defense of the Philippines under the terms of the 1947 Military Bases Agreement and the 1951 Mutual Defense Treaty. Although operational command and control of the Royal Brunei Armed Forces passed into Bruneian hands after the sultanate became a sovereign nation in 1984, a small corps of British and Commonwealth officers continues to be "on loan" for the more technical aspects of the military's mission. In addition, a British Army Gurkha Battalion has been stationed in Brunei since 1962 under the terms of a mutual defense agreement (Croissant and Lorenz 2018: 26).

Despite the multiethnic character of their societies, the militaries in Brunei, Malaysia, and Singapore – but not in the Philippines – have or still exhibit features of monoethnic armies. In Malaysia and Brunei, the armed forces are predominantly Malay forces, with a sizable component of noncitizens serving in the Brunei armed forces, and the Singapore Armed Forces were originally a Chinese-conscript military. In contrast, the AFP never became an ethnically based army mainly because there was no tradition of ethnopreferential recruitment during the American period. Furthermore, the Philippines is a minority-majority country, where no single ethnic group has a majority share of the total population or dominates the postcolonial political system. President Marcos prioritized promotions to officers from his home region of Ilocos in northwestern Luzon (Woo 2010). However, this did not amount to broad discrimination in recruitment.

In contrast to what the scholarship on civil–military relations conceives as "ethnic stacking" – the prioritization of officer promotions from the same

Table 6 Population Share of Largest Ethnic Group and Ethnopreferential
Military Recruitment

Country	Population share of largest ethnic group	Ethnopreferential recruitment
Brunei	65.7 percent	Yes (Malay)
Malaysia	60.8 percent (*Bumiputera*)[a]	Yes (Malay)
Philippines	28.1 percent	No
Singapore	74.3 percent	Yes (before 1977, Chinese)
Cambodia	97.6 percent	No
Indonesia	40.1 percent	No
Laos	53.2 percent	No
Myanmar	68.0 percent	Yes (Burman)
Timor-Leste	NA	No
Vietnam	85.7 percent	No
Thailand	97.5 percent	No

[a] *Bumiputera* (Malay for "sons of the soil") includes the indigenous peoples of Sabah and Sarawak in addition to Malays.

Source: *CIA World Factbook*; Croissant and Lorenz 2018.

minority ethnic group that supports a regime or a regime leader (Brown, Fariss, and McMahon 2016) – ethnopreferential military recruitment in Southeast Asia targets majority ethnic groups in the context of a plural society (see Table 6). It has been, and in some countries still is, a tool of state- and nation-building aimed at creating a military force loyal to the central government. As mentioned previously, initially after separating from Malaysia, Singaporean Malays were de facto excluded from conscription. In 1977, however, the government adopted an integration policy, and since then, all eligible Malays have been called up for national service, and some have received promotion to senior ranks (Tan 2001: 287; Chong and Chan 2017).

Ethnicity played an even more crucial part in shaping civil–military interactions in the plural society of Malaysia. The Malaysian Armed Forces have been a symbol of Malay nationhood since 1957, and ethnic Malays are heavily overrepresented in the military. The king, who is selected among the nine traditional Malay rulers, is supreme commander, and traditionally the chief of defense forces is a Malay (Beeson and Bellamy 2008: 83). In addition, no non-Malay has ever held the defense portfolio or the post of the home minister, who is responsible for police and security policy. Within the framework of the Alliance and the Barisan Nasional government, the United Malays National Organization (UMNO), the largest component party, had close personal and economic relations with military elites, who, after completing their service, often took influential positions in UMNO-controlled businesses (Crouch 1991: 127–29; Searle 1999: 83). As Muthiah Alagappa (1988:31) notes, the military became "a factor in the domestic inter-ethnic power equation but not by its own choice." It is rather a common interest of Malay elites in politics, business, civil service, and the armed forces to preserve Malay predominance, which provides strong incentives for the military to be a loyal servant of a Malay-led government.

Similarly, Singapore's military is part of a civilian-controlled security sector with a unified chain of command under a civilian-led ministry of defense. Government authority in routine questions is exercised through the civilian Armed Forces Council, whereas policy decisions are a domain of the Defense Council, which is led by the prime minister (Huxley 2000: 81).

Despite its small size, the city-state is one of the largest importers of military hardware worldwide; has become the main center for manufacturing, assembling, and servicing military material in the region; and possesses the best-equipped and well-trained military in Southeast Asia. Moreover, Singapore has also one of the largest militaries in the region in terms troops-to-citizen population ratio (1:48 in 2014) and has one of the largest defense budgets in terms of share of central government expenditures (29.6 percent in 2005; Bureau of Arms Control, Verification, and Compliance 2017).

Similar to other party-based autocracies in the region, there is a strong element of civil–military fusion in Singapore because the officers corps is a key recruitment pool for the city's administrative and political elite. The military education and promotion system encourages officers to acquire expertise in military and nonmilitary issues alike. Even during their active service, military officers are assigned to serve on statutory boards, administrative bodies, or universities to gather administrative experience or to continue their training (Huxley 2000: 232–34). These measures are meant to transition officers ending their active service in their late forties or early fifties into a career in the public service and have earned the armed services the label as a "civil service in uniform" (Peled 1995: 11).[8] However, unlike other party regimes such as Vietnam and Laos, there is strict institutional separation between the ruling party and the armed forces. Active military service personnel are barred from joining a political party and cannot run for political office. And in contrast to Southeast Asian countries with a praetorian military, the movement of active or retired military officers into civilian positions represents

---

[8] For example, in 2012, six of the then 15 members of the cabinet were former military officers, including Prime Minister Lee Hsien Loong (Barr 2014: 82).

the PAP's "efforts to create a common pool of national elites who can be deployed interchangeably in all institutional fields" (Tan 2011). Or, as Sean Walsh (2007: 272) notes, the "social and functional integration results in a partial civilianization of the military and ensures stable and effective civil–military relations."

The main differences between the civil–military relations in Malaysia and Singapore, on the one hand, and in Brunei, on the other, are first that in Brunei the control of the defense force is highly personalized. Both the small but modern and professional military and the Gurkha Reserve Unit, which is technically not part of the Royal Armed Forces, are under the personal authority of the sultan. Second, with the Gurkhas, the Bruneian military contains a substantial component of foreign recruits.

The armed forces and the Gurkha Reserve Unit play an important role in the oil-rich sultanate that only became a full sovereign state in January 1984. The centrality can be measured in terms of the personnel and the share of the state budget that these organizations absorb. Although the armed forces are only about 7,000 troops strong – the second smallest military force in Southeast Asia – the sultanate has the second highest troops-to-population ratio (1:52), and military expenditures as a percentage of central government expenditures (9.8 percent in 2005) are third highest in the region (cf. Bureau of Arms Control, Verification, and Compliance 2017).

Similar to Malaysia, the armed forces in Brunei are the embodiment of the Malay–Muslim identity of the nation. It is an all-voluntary force that only accepts citizens with a Malay ethnic background into its ranks. While essentially an external defense force with limited responsibilities in domestic security, the military provides support for the civilian government in disaster management and counterterrorism, as well as for counterinsurgency operations. In contrast, the Gurkha Reserve Unit, whose 400 to 2,000 troops and officers are former soldiers of British Gurkha Regiments, British officers, and retired members of the Singaporean police, is a regime security force. Its mission is to protect the Seria oil fields, the main source of income for the country, and the palace, public facilities, and government offices, as well as to serve as a parallel military force that is capable of countering threats to the sultan by the regular armed forces (Croissant and Lorenz 2018: 26–27).

The classification of the (pre–martial law) Philippines as a case of professional civil–military relations is perhaps controversial because the relationship between soldiers, state, and society in the Philippines passed through several stages since 1935. During the first phase from 1935 to 1965, the military was seasonally involved in socioeconomic and political functions and fought the

Huk peasant rebellion, but the supremacy of democratically elected authorities over the military was a key tenant of Philippine civil–military relations (see Section 2). Following the election of President Ferdinand Marcos and especially after the declaration of martial law on September 23, 1972, military participation in practically all areas of national and local affairs expanded dramatically. Soldiers were involved in policy implementation, assumed judicial roles as members of special military tribunals with authority over civilians, and managed civilian government agencies and private enterprises sequestered by the Marcos administration (Miranda and Ciron 1988: 174–77). Most important, however, Marcos replaced the old system of joint presidential and congressional oversight with his patrimonial control over the AFP. Through a combination of favoritism, expansion of the military budget and personnel, and a centralized command and control system with Marcos at its top, the president managed to subjugate the military and bend its leadership to his will (Hernandez 2006: 394). AFP personnel increased from 58,000 in 1972 to 157,000 in 1983. The military budget as share of gross national product (GNP) increased from 1.2 percent in 1964–65 to 1.9 percent in 1983, when the national debt crisis spiraled out of control, which forced the government to cut expenditures to 1.05 percent in 1985 (Miranda and Ciron 1988: 171; Bureau of Arms Control, Verification, and Compliance 2017). Marcos' strategy of recruiting the military as junior partner in his ruling coalition had far-reaching implications because it came at the expense of military cohesion and effectiveness. His promotion of politically loyal but inept army officers to senior posts and the attritional struggle against communist and Muslim rebels alienated many junior and midlevel officers from the political leadership and from their superiors inside the AFP (Celoza 1997: 79; Wurfel 1988: 237–40; Woo 2010: 375).

Marcos also attempted to keep the military in check by creating new centers of power headed by civilians who were wholly dependent on his favors. For this purpose, the dictator established his *Kilusang Bagong Lipunan* ("New Society Movement"), a political party with autonomy from the military, but it was politically and institutionally so weak that it proved utterly ineffective in checking the military's role and influence. Hence, when the Marcos government spiraled into crisis in 1985–86 as a consequence of economic decline and the rise of armed insurgencies, political mishaps, and anti-incumbent mass protests, the dictator came to rely completely on the military for his self-preservation (Slater 2010b).

On February 21, 1986, a small group of military officers (publically known as the Reform Armed Forces Movement) led by Marcos' civilian defense minister, Juan Ponce Enrile, and the AFP vice chief of staff, General Fidel

Ramos, attempted a coup against President Marcos. The attempt failed, but it catalyzed the "People Power" mass protests that brought down the dictator and triggered a transition to democracy (Thompson 1995).

The downfall of Marcos' personalist dictatorship marks the beginning of a new stage in the development of civil–military relations. At the core of post-Marcos civil–military relations in the Philippines was a double challenge for civilian actors (Croissant 2015). The first challenge concerned the inauguration of a democratic government without provoking military resistance. The second challenge was to establish functional institutions of civilian control over the military. Despite a wave of failed coup attempts between 1986 and 1989 and a series of lesser mutinies in the mid-2000s, Philippine democracy survived the first challenge. However, it was less successful in dealing with the second challenge. On the one hand, the 1987 constitution provides safeguards for effective democratic control, including the establishment of a Commission for Human Rights, the separation of police and military, the reestablishment of congressional oversight, and the incompatibility of active military service and holding political office. On the other hand, Presidents Fidel Ramos (1992–98) and Gloria Macapagal Arroyo (2001–10) relied heavily on co-opting military officers into the civilian government apparatus, appointing several dozen (former) military officers to advisory, cabinet, and administrative posts. The current president, Rodrigo Duterte (since 2016), is pushing to expand the role of the AFP in his "war on drugs" – a role that the military is neither prepared nor constitutionally mandated to fulfill. The ambivalent character of Filipino civil–military relations in the post–martial law era and the state of conditional submission of the armed forces under civilian control are aptly characterized by two Filipino political scientists, who note that the AFP "does not really seek to capture political power for itself (despite all the instances of attempted coups), and instead institutionally (through the upper ranks of the military leadership) aligns itself with certain political factions" (Hernandez and Kraft 2010: 130).

3.4 Neopatrimonial Civil–Military Relations

Cambodia and Timor-Leste are two of the most ambitious cases of postconflict peace-building and reconstruction under the aegis of United Nations–led international interim governments, yet these countries also demonstrate how a haphazard process of disarmament, demobilization, and reintegration of ex-combatants and ignoring the political nature of security sector reform can threaten the success of such programs and contribute to strong neopatrimonial features in civil–military relations.

Neopatrimonialism has been a key feature of Cambodian politics and civil–military relations under the governments of King Norodom Sihanouk (1955–70) and Marshal Lon Nol (1970–75), continued under the government of the pro-Vietnamese Cambodian People's Party (CPP) from 1979 to 1991, and has reemerged in the post-UN period since 1993. As part of the 1991 Paris Agreement between the Khmer warring parties that ended the civil war, the official military of the State of Cambodia and two of the three opposition armies[9] were integrated into the new Royal Cambodian Armed Forces. This resulted in a bloated military with more than 135,000 personnel, of which around 60 percent were former government troops, more officers than enlisted soldiers (Richardson and Sainsbury 2009: 289), but without a unified command.

The precarious transition from war to peace in Cambodia initially prevented Prime Minister Hun Sen of the CPP from assuming control of the security apparatus.[10] Lacking a unified command, the loyalties of individuals were determined by their political affiliation with the various civil war factions/ political parties (Var 2016: 251). This effectively meant that Hun Sen had no way of unilaterally controlling the armed forces in the early 1990s. Following the 1997 coup against Co-Prime Minister Prince Ranariddh, however, Hun Sen managed to gradually seize control not only of the armed forces but also of the national police and to establish a plethora of paramilitary units. Taken together, these armed organizations serve as Prime Minister Hun Sen's personal author-itarian tool to protect him from both popular revolt and internal coups (Chambers 2017: 197; Morgenbesser 2017).

While the regular military is led by officers who are connected to the government via family ties, as CPP members, or as clients of the high-ranking party cadres, there are a number of units that – in typical coup-proofing fashion – circumvent the chain of command and report directly to the prime minister. The most powerful unit is the heavily armed Prime Minister Bodyguard Unit, numbering around 10,000 troops. It serves as a counterweight to the regular army but is also used to monitor and intimidate the opposition and civil society (Croissant and Lorenz 2018).

Unlike other authoritarian regimes in the region, the regular military is not primarily meant to counter internal security threats or guarantee regime

---

[9] Khmer People's National Liberation Armed Forces and National Army of Independent Kampuchea; the Khmer Rouge army faction boycotted the DDR process.

[10] Hun Sen is a former Khmer Rouge military commander who deserted to Vietnam but returned to Cambodia in 1978–79 and rose through the ranks of the CPP to become prime minister in 1985. Following the national elections of 1993, which the CPP actually lost, Hun Sen threatened to resume fighting if he would not be granted the post of a second or co-prime minister, coequal to Prime Minister Prince Ranariddh of the FUNCINPEC Party.

security; this task is left to the police (controlled by the minister of interior), the military police, the gendarmerie (reporting directly to the prime minister), domestic intelligence, the Bodyguard Unit, and violent youth organizations such as the "Pagoda Boys" (Chambers 2015). Rather, the armed forces constitute a huge spoils network that is fueled by the defense budget, spending for internal security, and corruption (Chambers 2015; Morgenbesser 2017). Although there is no genuine military business complex, senior army, military police, and police officers are all involved in illegal activities, including illegal logging and land grabbing (see Section 4).

While UN efforts in security-sector reform in Cambodia focused on the military, in Timor-Leste, the United Nations focused on the police (Myrttinen 2012). The creation and recruitment of the Falinitil-Forças de Defesa de Timor-Leste (F-FDTL) was left to the discretion of Falintil, the military wing of the Timorese national resistance movement against the occupation by Indonesia. As a result, most of the recruits for the new army were ex-combatants, mostly from the eastern parts (Loro Sae) of the country, whereas the national police (Polícia Nacional de Timor-Leste) was mostly comprised of former Timorese members of the Indonesian police from the western (Loro Munu) districts (Kammen 2013: 111).

When former resistance leaders and the main resistance-legacy political parties began to use existing fissures and cleavages within the F-FDTL and between army and police for their own political purposes, both institutions quickly became embroiled in political struggles between the president and the government led by the Fretilin Party (Sahin and Feaver 2013), and combined with conflicts over scarce resources, relations between the two services became hostile. Tensions escalated in April 2006, when fighting between army and police troops and civil unrest in the capital of Dili resulted in more than 30 deaths and 150,000 internally displaced persons. The breakdown of public order could only be averted through the deployment of an "International Stabilization Force" of about 3,000 troops (Croissant 2008).

Since then, a series of institutional reforms – including new laws on national and internal security, a defense law, and the creation of a ministry for defense and security that integrates military and the police – has aimed at improving coordination and cooperation between police and armed forces. Still, occasional clashes between individuals from the police and the military suggest that there are problems of discipline, professionalism, and impartiality of both the police and the army (Sahin and Feaver 2013). Furthermore, the government policy of buying the loyalty of potential conflict spoilers, such as self-declared veterans of the independence struggle, armed militias, or violent youth gangs, has also had an impact on the professionalism and neutrality of the security services, especially given the precarious state of public revenues and the state budget. The budget for the F-FDTL increased from US$15.8 million in 2005 to US$55.5 million in 2009 (2015: US$37 million), and the size of the security forces (F-FDTL and police) has more than doubled since 2008. This was made possible by new oil and gas revenues in the billions of dollars per year that the government received from rapidly increasing production and prices from 2008 to 2012. Around 78 percent of the state budget for 2017 was derived from the petroleum sector, although oil and gas revenue are in decline, and the only producing gas field is expected to dry up by 2020 (Croissant and Lorenz 2018).

4 Military Roles: Old and New

The starting point in any analysis of military roles and missions is the nature of the perceived threat. For traditional civil–military relations in the West, the basic threat was seen as an enemy invasion, and the basic mission was territorial defense. However, in most of Southeast Asia, the dominant threat perception was and still is internal. Thus, in most cases, Southeast Asian armies have traditionally been internal security forces, and they focused on the broadly defined mission of safeguarding internal and regime security against armed separatists, communists insurgencies, and nonviolent opposition movements and furthering "national development," including infrastructure improvements, developing economic industries, and providing security and development assistance in lieu of the state (Alagappa 1988). Even though external missions such as multinational peace and stability operations have increased in recent years, external defense is the quintessential task only for the armed forces in Singapore, Malaysia (after 1971), and Brunei.

4.1 State- and Nation-Building

Most of the state- and nation-building in Southeast Asia must be situated within the historical context of the global wave of decolonization following World War II. During this phase of radical change and political turmoil, the armed forces emerged to different extents as catalyzers of state- and nation-building. In Burma and Indonesia, armed conflicts accompanied state-building, which were fought by paramilitary forces that were later incorporated into the states' regular militaries. The pivotal role of new militaries in liberation war and in quelling rebellions and dissident movements provided the fundament for military occupation of civilian positions and for soldiers' self-perception as the prime guarantors of national unity and the state's last (or only) line of defense against separatist threats and communist subversion.

However, their methods for maintaining national unity were largely counter-productive. The counterinsurgency wars in Aceh, Timor-Leste, and Papua, for example, exacerbated the sense of alienation from Indonesia that the people in these provinces already felt (Roosa 2007). Similarly, the Tatmadaw's pursue of violent state-building strategies created a gulf between the military institution and the broader society it purported to protect. While the brutal way of fighting internal wars served as legitimation for the political clout of the Tatmadaw, it failed to create national unity (Callahan 2005).

In socialist Vietnam and Laos, armies played a critical role in socialist state-building. But, in contrast to Indonesia and Myanmar, soldiers did perform such functions under the primacy and guidance of the ruling Party. After the collapse of the royalist government in 1975, the Lao Communist Party framed the role of the People's Army in terms of "two strategic tasks" (Dwyer 2014: 387): defending the new socialist republic against external and internal enemies and simultaneously performing key functions in postwar reconstruction and building socialism. Similarly in (North) Vietnam, the core function of the People's Army was national revolution and socialist reconstruction. Because the "enemy" was internal (i.e., bourgeoisie, capitalist class, feudal lords) *and* external (i.e., the United States), this meant that the army had both internal and external threat perceptions (Thayer 2003).

Under the dictatorship of Field Marshal Plaek Phibunsongkhram, from 1937 to 1944 and 1948 to 1957, the Thai military had a key role in developing a new Thai nationalist identity called *kwampenthai* ("Thai-ness" or "being Thai") defined by the trinity of one nation, one religion (Buddhism), and one shared history embodied in the person of the king. Yet, even in periods during which the Thai armed forces did not act as the subordinate to the palace, the military exploited the monarchy's symbolic power and legitimacy for its own role as nation-building architect (Rappa 2017).

For reasons mentioned previously, soldiers played a secondary or even marginal role in the conceptualization and construction of the nation-state and nationalist identities in presocialist Cambodia, Laos, and South Vietnam, the Philippines, and the former British colonies of Brunei, Malaysia, and Singapore. When military institutions became an embodiment of a particular understanding of national identity, as in Malaysia and Brunei, they did so not by their own choice.

4.2 Organization and Exercise of Political Domination

Up to the present, there is no country in Southeast Asia where the civil military relations correspond to the normative model of democratic civil–military relations, which is based on the assumption of an institutional separation between one civilian sphere and one military sphere and in which the armed forces are the servant of a democratically legitimized principal.

Even in those political regimes where there is a formal separation between the civilian institutions and the military, there is often an informal fusion of both spheres at the elite level. Moreover, one of the main insights of Section 3 is that even when the transition from authoritarian government to a democratic political regime succeeded, as in the Philippines, Indonesia, and Timor-Leste, the institutionalization of democratic civilian control has remained incomplete. In Indonesia, democratic reforms since the turn of the century have gone hand-in-hand with greater professionalization and political control without fully overcoming the deeply ingrained patterns of decades of military meddling in politics (Honna 2017; Mietzner 2018). In the Philippines, the transition from authoritarianism to democracy triggered an outburst of military praetorianism, with a series of six coup attempts between 1986 and 1990. And in Timor-Leste, security-sector reform as part of UN-led efforts in postconflict reconstruction and democratization have not resulted in better democratic governance of the security sector but rather created factionalized neopatrimonial security forces, including a fragile military.

However, it is necessary to differentiate the participation of national armies in regime formation from their role in the exercise of political power afterwards. In Burma, Indonesia, South Vietnam, and Thailand, the armed forces had a pivotal role in the creation, exercise, and defense of authoritarian rule. In all these cases, as well as in Cambodia (1970), military elites organized coups d'état that led to the formation of military-controlled governments. Yet Thai politicomilitary leaders – other than Phibunsongkhram and Sarit Thanarat, who had deposed Phibunsongkhram in a coup in 1957 and served as prime minister until his death in 1963 – never alone wielded quite the same degree of political and military control as Ne Win in Burma or Suharto in Indonesia enjoyed. Unlike them, Thai military leaders lacked the charisma or desire to forge an independent political movement centered around their person and, equally important, had to be considerate of other intramilitary factions that were competing with them over power and influence. In addition, the Thai king also played a more determinate role, highly visible in picking sides in the military coups of 1976 and 1981 and the struggle between protestors and government in 1973, 1992, 2005, and 2010 (Handley 2006; Hewison and Kengkij 2010).

While in Thailand and Burma the military remains the impetus behind the government rather than a parallel or subordinate force, the military under Marcos and during the final years of Suharto's rule became a countervailing influence after being successfully sidelined by the dictators. Although the military remained influential until the end of Suharto's rule and provided a key function for regime security as it conducted counterinsurgency campaigns and antiopposition operations, both the Indonesian and Filipino military fulfilled a supporting rather than a ruling role. The same is true for the Cambodian military under Hun Sen's personalist rule.

In Cambodia and the Philippines, military elites who backed the dictator received rewards in the form of privileged access to state spoils and government positions, but soldiers did not have the means to advance to become the leading political force in the two regimes. Hun Sen, especially, has intensely fractured the national coercive institutions and fostered the development of dual structures within the military and security apparatus. Similar to other Cambodian rulers, Hun Sen appreciates personal loyalty more than military performance or professional merits. Parallel to the regular army, Hun Sen maintains multiple armed units for the repression of internal political dissent and to deter potential military coup plotters and has allotted key leadership positions to members of his own family.

In socialist Southeast Asia, military force was a key to establishing and enforcing Party rule, and the military is the last line of defense against "counterrevolutionary" threats. The socialist soldier, however, is politically dependent on the vanguard Party, and the structural integration of military elites into the Party apparatus was combined with political dependency and unequal partnership. With the introduction of market economic reforms in the 1980s and geopolitical shifts in the 1990s, the communist soldiers adapted to a new role as "socialist entrepreneurs" (Stuart-Fox 2009: 162), but the military has by no means become the most influential political actor (Thayer 2017: 130–31).

Finally, the armed forces in Singapore, Brunei, and Malaysia had no meaningful role to play in the formation of political regimes and were not involved in the daily maintenance of regime security. The prerequisites for the military's marginal political role were the formation of relatively strong nonmilitary political organizations and civilian institutions still under colonial rule, the exclusion of members of the military from the political sphere, limited military capabilities and a relatively effective mix of ideological and performance-based legitimacy, co-optation of key elites, and low-intensity repression, which is a domain of police and judiciary (Croissant and Lorenz 2018).

4.3 Revolutions and Regime Transitions

Even as the patterns of military intervention into politics have changed over time, the military in Myanmar and Thailand still occupies the role of a political ruler, dominating the regime coalition and steering the political process – either overtly or behind a civilianized facade. In contrast, in the authoritarian orders of Indonesia, the Philippines, and contemporary Cambodia, as well as in Laos and Vietnam, the role of soldiers was (or still is) to assist the political leaders in exercising political power.

Obviously, such variations matter. A more powerful military is more effective in repressing political dissent and conflict, but at the same time it is in a better position to demand political and economic concessions in exchange for its role in maintaining the regime (Svolik 2012). In contrast, where authoritarian governments and autocratic rulers employ strategies of political control that discriminate between a small group of loyalist officers who receive preferential treatment for promotions and opportunities for enrichment, they create winners and losers inside the military, which can become an important source of intramilitary conflict and may undermine military support for the regime during times of crisis (Lee 2015).

Although most countries in the region are not democracies, Southeast Asia experienced its own share of popular movements demanding regime change (but not necessarily achieving it) and regime transitions, including the Philippines, Burma, Thailand, Cambodia, Indonesia, and Timor-Leste (Shin and Tusalem 2009). With the exception of Cambodia and Timor-Leste, where UN-led interim governments monitored the transition to democracy, authoritarian rulers in these countries confronted nonviolent mass mobilizations. However, popular protests against the dictator triggered very different reactions among military officers, with important consequences for the outcomes of the protests in terms of actual leader and regime changes. In the Philippines and Indonesia, military defection was the tipping point that opened the door for a transition to democracy. In Myanmar, military repression in August–September 1988 ushered a new military-led government – the SLORC – into office. Similarly, Thailand's National Peace Keeping Council, a military junta led by Army Chief Suchinda Kraprayoon that overthrew the civilian government of Prime Minister Chavalit in early 1991, decided to use lethal force against peaceful demonstrations in Bangkok in May 1992. This created a backlash of antigovernment outrage, resulting in King Bhumibol Adulyadej stepping in and forcing Suchinda to resign (LoGorfo 1997).

In the Philippines, the Reform Armed Forces Movement led by Marcos' civilian defense minister, Juan Ponce Enrile, and the AFP vice chief of staff, General Fidel Ramos, staged a coup d'état on February 22, 1986. The coup attempt failed but catalyzed the "People Power" (or EDSA) mass protests against Marcos and a "cascade of defections" (Lee 2009: 653) among AFP personnel and civilian elites.[11] In contrast, in Indonesia, military defection from the dictator occurred as a reaction to noncooperation among protestors and civilian insiders of the Suharto regime. Faced with widespread popular unrest, some military hardliners advocated cracking down on the protests. However, moderate elites within Golkar and General Wiranto, commander of the Indonesian Armed Forces, asked Suharto to step down in order to subdue economic and social upheaval (Mietzner 2009: 126). Facing a crumbling regime coalition and opposition from within the highest ranks of the armed forces, Suharto yielded on May 21, 1998, and transferred power to his vice president, Bacharuddin Jusuf Habibie, which marks the beginning of the *reformasi* period.

The key reason why Southeast Asian militaries reacted so differently to anti-incumbent mass demonstrations was the character of the military organization itself and its relationship with regime leaders (Kim 2008; Lee 2015). As already established in Section 2, the Thai military was traditionally one of the most factionalized military organizations in the region. However, before the 1991 coup, officers from the Chulachomkalo Military Academy Class 5 had managed to occupy key positions in the army hierarchy. Most of the coup leaders and members of the National Peace Keeping Council belonged to this faction (LoGorfo 1997). Based on the ease with which Suchinda was able to remove key officers from their positions following the 1991 coup, it can be assumed that his faction had full control over key military units (Lee 2015). Similarly, Burma's failure to democratize in 1988–90 was not due to the weakness of civil society but because of the strength and internal cohesion of the Tatmadaw, and the collapse of the regime party during the 1988 uprising cleared the way for the military to reassert its prerogatives. The key difference between the two cases, however, was that in the emerging stalemate between Thailand's military council and the democracy movement, there was a third power, the king, who possessed the authority to demand an end to the confrontation.

In contrast, President Suharto, as shown in Section 3, had sought to rein in the army by fundamentally centralizing the military's command structures into his hands and by consistently filling all the key command positions within the armed forces with officers that he handpicked (Lee 2015). Suharto's style of managing the military could be considered highly effective in proofing his rule

---

[11] As Montiel (2010: 176) notes, for most civilians, the demise of Marcos signaled the triumph for a civilian-based, nonviolent protest movement, whereas the military storyline "is one of an aborted coup that was spearheaded by idealistic and disgruntled officers ... that highlights the pivotal role taken by the military's withdrawal of support from the Marcos dictatorship." The competing narratives of who "owned" the revolution explain, to some degree, the antagonistic civilian–military relations in the immediate post-EDSA period.

against the risk of another military coup. However, it also created fissures and conflicts within the officer corps. Factional tensions within the armed forces were especially manifest between officers who benefited in terms of career opportunities, income, and prestige from Suharto's divide-and-rule strategy and those who did not. Due to its factionalized state, the military was unable to muster a coherent voice on how to best deal with the student demonstrators and what to do to preserve the regime (Lee 2009).

As noted previously, Marcos' strategy of consolidating his personal control over the Philippine military had far-reaching implications because it came at the expense of military professionalism and cohesion and created factional competition within the AFP (Wurfel 1988: 237–40). It also led to the formation of the Reform the Armed Forces Movement, composed of junior and middle-ranking officers who agitated against corruption in the armed forces, promotions based on favoritism, and overstaying generals who blocked the younger generation's career opportunities (Kim 2008: 41).

In this regard, it is important to note that the ruling parties in Singapore, Malaysia, Laos, and Vietnam have established patterns of government control over the military that do *not* create the kind of intramilitary fissure that made the autocratic rulers in Indonesia and the Philippines vulnerable to shifting elite loyalties and military defection. Despite the many differences in the systems of political–military relations, ruling parties in these four countries succeeded in establishing forms of civil–military interaction that stress the cooperation of elites in the armed forces and the ruling party/parties because their specific interests converged toward the same national goals and secured the integration of military elites into the broader elite structure of the authoritarian order.

The developments in Cambodia point in the opposite direction, with political leader Hun Sen weakening established party mechanisms of political oversight and co-optation in an effort to personalize control over the military establishment. Hun Sen used the military as a mechanism to co-opt regime elites but relied on other armed groups to ensure regime security against elite splits and mass unrest. However, the co-optation of the Cambodian military in the power structure of an increasingly personalist dictatorship depended much more on the continuous ability of the ruler to reward loyal behavior than on shared political values, ideologies, or conceptions of "good" civil–military relations. Moreover, as Terence Lee (2015: 4) notes with regard to the Philippines and Indonesia, increasing patrimonialism and personalism within the armed forces can lead to political dissensions between military officers competing for better positions in the regime. However, "when popular demonstrations emerged, personalism created apt conditions for the defections of disaffected senior officers."

4.4 Military Entrepreneurship

One aspect that is emblematic of the more complex roles of Southeast Asian militaries compared with their counterparts in the West and in most other regions is that in the post–World War II period, soldiers organized in some cases military business complexes and became commercial actors with wide-ranging influence and impact on their national economies. Kristina Mani (2011: 184–85) defines *military entrepreneurship* as "the military's ownership, management or stakeholding of economic enterprises [and] the innovative creation of resources and means of production by commissioned military officers acting in an institutional capacity as formal owners, managers and stakeholders of enterprises that generate financial resources or goods directly benefiting the military. Their activities are generally legal [although illicit activities are included] and politically sanctioned, though not necessarily just or transparent." This definition bears a range of collective and individual activities, both informal and institutionalized. Yet they all have inherent political implications in common: as businessmen, soldiers can secure for themselves significant sources of revenue that do not depend on government appropriation. Hence, for militaries, entrepreneurship is a potentially powerful means to enhance their autonomy from civilian control and even to exert influence within the state and society.

However, the most frequently asked questions about military businesses in Southeast Asia and elsewhere – their exact size, how much profit they generate, and their proportion of the national economy – are almost impossible to answer. Military business complexes are opaque, and military enterprises are often untaxed and unaudited by either the parliament or public accountability agencies (Abul-Magd 2017). Finally, it is no secret that the countries with the greatest military control over economic resources are often also the ones with least open and transparent political regimes.

Generally, it has to be assumed that "businessmen in arms" (Grewert and Abul-Magd 2016) do not operate under "normal" market conditions. Hence military businesses often suffer from problems of corruption, moral hazard, and inefficient or misuse of funds, personnel, resources, or equipment. Military entrepreneurship is also potentially harmful to the achievement or maintenance of military effectiveness, especially when a substantial part of the armed forces is directly engaged in such activities as a more or less daily routine (Brömmelhörster and Paes 2003: 16).

Regarding types of military entrepreneurship in Southeast Asia, three clusters of countries can be identified. A first group comprises the cases of Thailand, Indonesia, and Myanmar. Here the commercialization of military establishments was already evident in the 1950s (Hoadley 1975: 156). Military economic actors engaged in a broad range of commercial and profit-making activities, from developing corporations, welfare foundations (known as *yayasan* in Indonesia), and even unit-level commercial operations and selling their coercive power for money.

Second, the transition of a developing socialist economy to a mixed, multi-sector economy since the 1980s provided the political–ideological framework for military entrepreneurship and also became an important element of economic and military modernization in Laos and Vietnam. Even though military economic involvement in Vietnam and Laos was not altogether new, what is novel are the market operations of military units.

The third cluster consists of countries in which economic and commercial roles of the military are minor or absent, as in Singapore, Malaysia, Brunei, and Timor-Leste. This group also includes the Philippines, where the profit-making activities of soldiers are primarily for their individual spoils and are embedded in shadow economies of local conflict zones, and Cambodia, where soldiers participate in the spoils of a kleptocratic regime by selling their coercive power.

What drove the rise of military entrepreneurship in the countries of the first and second clusters was a complex combination of material, ideological, and political factors (cf. Mani 2011: 184): first, a *critical economic juncture*, which triggered an examination of national economic priorities in the armed forces; second, the *military's strategic ideological priorities*, which conditioned the kind of entrepreneurship soldiers were pursuing; and third, *coalitional opportunities* the military encountered with state or private-sector actors, which provided the degree of legitimacy the military needed to acquire military enclaves. In contrast, militaries in the third cluster lacked the kind of structural, political, and cultural factors that motivated and enabled militaries of the first and second clusters to become businessmen.

Businessmen in Arms

Myanmar stands out as the one case in Southeast Asia where the military is the most significant single player in the national economy. Already in 1951, the army's Defense Services Institute expanded to take over major import-export operations for the whole country. In the 1960s, through the government's nationalization program under the military's pseudosocialist ideology, the Tatmadaw successfully established a virtual monopoly over the economic activities of the nation (Selth 2002: 146). Every major ministry, commission, and public corporation was headed by a military man, while civilian bureaucrats continued to staff the lower ranks of the bureaucracy (Hoadley 1975: 58).

In this respect, Burma under the rule of Ne Win and his military peers differed significantly from Thailand and Indonesia. Military rulers in Thailand and Indonesia seemed to have appreciated the civilian bureaucracy's importance to some extent, seeing it as a political counterweight to the military and acknowledging the superior qualifications of civilian technocrats in drafting economic policies. In Burma, in contrast, Ne Win reduced state agencies to "medieval fiefdoms" (Yawnghwe 1997: 97). As a consequence, the bureaucracy withered, and mismanagement and erratic policy decisions drove the country into widespread poverty and economic despair.

The year 1988, however, marked a caesura in the evolution of the Tatmadaw's economic role. The State Law and Order Restoration Council recognized the shortcomings of the old socialist practices and introduced a number of economic changes that ended the socialist experiment but enabled the Tatmadaw to consolidate its control of the nation's economic base through purely commercial operations (Selth 2002: 146). As a result, the 1990s saw the creation and expansion of a number of military-owned conglomerates, such as the Union of Myanmar Economic Holdings Limited and the Myanmar Economic Corporation, and private companies owned by military officers or their civilian cronies (Bünte 2017: 117–18). Furthermore, a new "ceasefire capitalism" (Woods 2011) emerged in the periphery, where ethnic armed groups, warlords, military commanders, and local entrepreneurs of violence engaged and cooperated in a vast range of commercial interests and enterprises. Despite economic reforms under the Thein Sein government (2011–16), Myanmar so far has not overcome this legacy of military entrepreneurship. In fact, the Burmese economy is still very much under control of businessmen in arms and their civilian clients who are the main (and sometimes only) beneficiaries of the transition to rentier capitalism (Lall 2016: 43).

From its earliest days, the Indonesian armed forces depended primarily on their own economic activities for survival and political relevance. As mentioned in Section 2, the economic activities of the military had roots in the guerrilla warfare against Dutch colonial ambitions in the post–World War II period. Yet the institutionalization of the military's entrepreneurial role began in earnest in 1957 with the declaration of martial law by Sukarno (McCulloch 2003: 122). The nationalization of Dutch, British, and American companies under Sukarno and the change in economic policies after the transition from Sukarno to Suharto allowed military elites to take over control of some of the new state-owned enterprises, and different service branches and special forces established foundations as holding companies for their business interests (Mietzner and Misol 2012). These corporate units provided not only wealth but also a political power base. Many military businesses remained small, but others, such as those in the petroleum sector, grew and became critical sources of funding for the military's projects during the oil boom of the 1970s and 1980s (Brown 2006: 961). Moreover, the military's engagement in armed conflicts in Aceh and West Papua – regions with high resource endowments – enabled military commanders, in collaboration with military-assisted corporations, to control natural resource extraction (Brown 2006: 961–62).

The *dwifungsi* doctrine and territorial command and Suharto's authoritarian "New Order" corporatism bestowed the ideological legitimation and political opportunity for the armed forces to develop their stakes in some of the most lucrative sectors of the national economy, such as fishing, finance, real estate, manufacturing, and construction. Yet many military enterprises suffered from corruption, waste, and mismanagement, which led to compulsory restructuring and reductions with heavy losses.[12] Democratic reforms after 1998 have also put pressure on the military to hand over business activities owned and operated by military units to the government and to make their economic activities more accountable to parliament, the president, and public accountability agencies. So far these efforts have had limited impact and left the large field of informal military fund-raising untouched (Mietzner and Misol 2012; Honna 2017: 317).

In Thailand, it was essentially during the premierships of Plaek Phibunsongkhram and especially Sarit Thanarat that an impenetrable complex of military-run businesses inside and outside the state emerged (Chambers and Waitoolkiat 2017). So-called commercial soldiers set up their own business firms, secured control over state-owned enterprises and semigovernment companies, and gained free shares from private firms owned mainly by Sino-Thai businessmen, thereby establishing their own economic base (Samudavanija 1982: 14). This, in turn, transformed the "professional army officers corps into politico-economic interest groups [who] were primarily concerned with political-economic power and status more than the 'corporate interest' or 'professionalism' of the Armed Forces" (Samudavanija 1982: 18–19).

After 1957, Field Marshal Sarit emphasized economic development to provide legitimacy and justification for his personalist rule. In reaction to the rapidly deteriorating security situation in Laos and at the urging of the United States, for which Thailand became more important as Washington became more engaged in Indochina, Sarit's interest in economic development took a security orientation (Kraisoraphong 2014: 79). Sarit, his military clique, and the monarchy profited from US financial and military aid and business

---

[12] The volume and size of the military's business empire are impossible to gauge, and the contribution to the national economy is impossible to estimate. In 2003, Lesley McCulloch (2003: 122) gave a conservative estimate of about 3 percent of GDP.

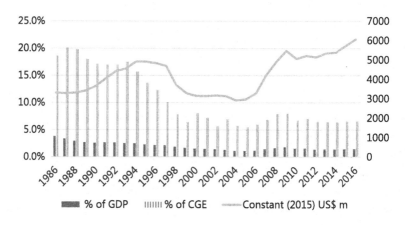

Figure 2 Military expenditure in Thailand, 1986–2016
Source: SIPRI 2017.

investments coming from the United States. The military government was the gatekeeper to economic development and financial growth in the country. At the same time, the monarchy regained all its financial assets and was allowed to pursue, mainly through the Crown Property Bureau, its own business ventures (von der Mehden 1970). In the 1960s, the Thai army assumed a direct role in development efforts in critical areas in the Northeast. This was extended to North and South Thailand after 1968. Finally, in the 1980s, traditional security-related development efforts were upgraded under the integrated strategic development program, which focused on selected strategic areas to defeat the communist insurgency (Alagappa 1988: 21). Yet the developmental role of the army remained miniscule and symbolic when compared with the total national development effort.

In the 1990s, military businessmen felt stronger pressure to reduce their economic clout. During this time, military involvement in commercial enterprises declined, and new regulations concerning broadcasting media in the 1997 constitution threatened the military's stakes in the nation's profitable telecommunications sector (Croissant et al. 2013: 161; Chambers and Waitoolkiat 2017: 53–54). Moreover, the military experienced significant budget cuts, especially in response to the 1997 Asian financial crisis (see Figure 2).

In 2001, incoming Prime Minister Thaksin Shinawatra attempted to personalize control over military financing and to carve a faction from the military and police that would be primarily loyal to him. In an effort to co-opt the military, Thaksin lifted the embargo on military procurements that had been in place since the 1997 financial crisis and summarily approved the entire army's spending list for the 2005–13 period. Thaksin also redistributed economic benefits from military businesses and the privatization of military-owned companies to military loyalists (McCargo and Pathmanand 2005).

As Figure 2 shows, though, following the 2006 and 2014 coups, the trend decrease in government military spending has been reversed. Since the coup in May 2014, the budget in the defense realm increased, while the Thai economy continues to struggle and other areas, such as education, saw significant decreases. Moreover, postcoup military councils have again strengthened military representation in public organizations, boards, and state-owned enterprises and sponsored legislation that grant economic concessions to military vested interests, for instance, in the telecommunications sector (Chambers and Waitoolkiat 2017: 51–65).

Socialist Entrepreneurs

It has already been established that in Laos and Vietnam, as a consequence of guerilla warfare and the need for self-sufficiency of military units, there was a tradition of military ownership and management of enterprises that could support both soldiers' needs and the political agenda of the Communist Revolution. Yet the adoption of "new economic measures" in Laos in 1985 and Vietnam's *doi moi* reforms in 1986 provided the political–ideological framework for the commercialization of the two militaries.

In Vietnam, the shift to a market-oriented economic system in the 1980s turned the People's Army in a multi-billion-dollar business. As Carlyle Thayer (2017: 130–31) notes, "by the mid-1990s the military's role in running civilian enterprises had become so extensive that two waves of reform (1995–97 and 1998–2006) were carried out to restructure these enterprises to make them more efficient and profitable." Since 1997, military-owned enterprises have been categorized as (Thayer 2017: 144) (1) defense economic enterprises whose main purpose is to produce or repair military equipment but also produce commercial goods as a sideline, (2) national defense economic enterprises that mostly produce and trade civilian products and services and are involved in economic development in remote areas, and (3) exclusive economic enterprises that specialize in manufacturing and trading in commercial products.

Vietnam's defense budget is a state secret. According to expert assessments, actual defense spending is much higher than officially announced figures. Nevertheless, experts agree that Vietnam has experienced defense retrenchment since the late 1980s, reflecting a mix of different influences: the end of the Cambodia intervention, the drop in foreign military aid by the Soviet Union and other communist countries of Eastern Europe, and a shrinking economy in the late 1980s. According to the International Institute for Security Studies (IISS) in London, defense spending declined in relative terms from 19.4 percent of GDP in 1989 to 2.01 percent in 2016. In comparison with 1985, military personnel strength was reduced by more than half by 2005 (IISS 2017).[13]

In order to compensate the People's Army for its shrinking budget and to free up resources for military modernization, military units gained permission to engage in commercial activities, and its enterprises were put on the same legal footing as state-owned enterprises (Thayer 2003; Vasavakul 2001: 354).

There are no comprehensive official figures on the contribution of military-owned enterprises to the national economy. Official estimates put their accrued total revenue at nearly 7 percent of GDP and their contribution to the state budget at 14 percent of total revenue (Thayer 2017: 153). They conduct business domestically, in neighboring countries such as Cambodia and Laos, as well as oversees (Thayer 2013: 75). Inside Vietnam, the Vietnamese People's Army controls economic security zones in geographically remote but strategically important areas where soldiers and their families live (Thayer 2013: 73, 82).

There are also many facets to the Lao military's role in the national economy. The most prominent are direct management of natural resources (especially timber), military ownership of commercial enterprises, and the involvement of military offices in private business ventures and commercial activities (Dwyer, Ingalls, and Baird 2016). With the second five-year plan (1986–91), the Lao People's Army became strongly involved in various sectors of the economy, including infrastructure and construction projects, mining, agriculture, forestry, fuel distribution, export-import, and tourism (Stuart-Fox 2002: 243; Stuart-Fox 2006: 61–62). While there is no reliable information on the concrete size and economic value of the military's business complex, most observers agree that commercial activities and military-owned enterprises are actually the main source of income for impoverished military officers. Military-owned enterprises – sometimes in collaboration with local businessmen, corrupt party cadres, or companies owned by the Vietnamese military – control vast parts of the logging and mining industries and conduct illicit border trade between Laos and Vietnam, China, and Myanmar (Hodgdon 2008; Baird 2010). It is also no secret that active-duty troops and decommissioned military personnel with patronage links have been working as private security for Vietnamese companies that are increasingly obtaining land concessions from

---

[13] This does not include civil defense, reserves and auxiliary forces, paramilitaries, dual-propose forces such as military and civilian police, military research and development, or income generated by military-owned enterprises.

the Lao government, resulting in the displacement of many rural farmers in southern Laos (Lipp and Chambers 2017).

Arms with No Business and Petty Kleptocrats

The third cluster of countries with no formally or informally institutionalized military business complex consists of five countries. In Malaysia, Singapore, the Philippines, Timor Leste, and Brunei, the military establishment lacks nonbudgetary or commercial sources of income. Even as the Malaysian government, as a reaction to intercommunal riots in 1969 ("May 13th Incident"), envisioned more direct military participation in the implementation of development policies and set up a series of institutions designed to provide formal channels for military officers to participate in policymaking on development issues (Ahmad 1988), this did not transform the armed forces into a commercial actor.

Similarly, the AFP, despite its role in socioeconomic development since the 1950s and many decades of military participation in "shadow economies of conflict zones" (Hall 2017: 277), has traditionally been unable to secure independent sources of revenue (Beeson and Bellamy 2008) and only very limited access to public allocations outside the regular appropriation or extrabudgetary revenues (Hall 2017: 285). However, under the new, "holistic" counterinsurgency approach of President Gloria Macapagal Arroyo (2001–10), so-called civil–military operation activities (focused on small-scale infrastructure projects and socioeconomic activities) received a boost (Hall 2017: 289–90). In contrast, decades of counterinsurgency operations in various parts of the archipelago and an intense focus on internal security have taken their toll on the AFP's overall military capabilities, and the AFP has earned the unsavory label of being one of the most poorly equipped forces in Southeast Asia. Under the administration of President Fidel Ramos (1992–98), the Philippines began an ambitious modernization program to transform the AFP into a conventional armed force comparable with most Southeast Asian militaries (and prepare for a shift from internal security and constabulary operations to its new primary focus on territorial defense and external missions). Yet this did not result in the modernization and reorientation of the AFP, most importantly because it added more mission areas for the AFP without providing adequate long-term funding (Hall 2017: 280). Unsurprisingly, the combination of mission creep and fiscal neglect has deteriorated military effectiveness, as demonstrated during the five-month battle for Marawi City between government troops and armed terror groups in 2017 (Tigno 2018).

Finally, the post-1993 military in Cambodia is somewhat a deviant case. The neopatrimonial regime of Prime Minister Hun Sen, in which corruption, co-optation, and (violent) resource extortion are the lifeblood of the political system and the glue for regime survival, provides a fertile environment for corrupt and illicit economic activities among soldiers. According to various reports, senior army, military police, and police officers are all heavily involved in illegal activities, including illegal logging, land grabbing, and contraband trafficking, whereas the lower ranks try to bolster their pay by engaging in the private security sector, drug or small-arms trade, prostitution, and racketeering. Military officers and enlisted soldiers complement their meager salaries by serving as bodyguards for individuals or selling their services to corporations in need of protection for their investments (Chambers 2017: 186). There are some military development zones, military institutional holdings, and holdings by individual security force commanders, and powerful military figures invest heavily in economic activities (Chambers 2017: 186), but these are not part of a broader military business complex or syndrome of institutionalized military entrepreneurship. Rather, the commercialization of the military is epiphenomenal on the kleptocratic and abusive character of state, regime, and economy, organized and controlled by top political elites, who raid state resources with immunity and impunity.

5 Conclusions and Outlook

At the onset of this Element, three sets of questions were posed, namely: Why did certain types of military organizations emerge in the late colonial and early postcolonial periods, and how did the role of new armies in the process of state- and nation-building affect civil–military relations in the new nation-states of Southeast Asia? What have been the roles and missions of Southeast Asian militaries, and how have they changed from independence until today? What types of civil–military relations emerged, and what are the main factors that explain change and continuity in the interactions between soldiers, state, and society?

5.1 The Formation of States, Nations, and Armies

As in other regions of the world, the formation of sovereign nation-states in Southeast Asia resulted in the creation of national armed forces. In Indonesia, Myanmar, and North Vietnam, anticolonial guerilla units formed the core of the new militaries. Similarly, most first-generation recruits for the Timor-Leste Defense Force were reintegrated ex-guerillas. In contrast, in Malaysia, the Philippines, and Brunei, national armies originated from colonial militaries and retained close connections with the former colonial powers. In anticom-munist Indochina, France and, later, the United States helped shape militaries and civil–military relations, but after anticommunist regimes had been defeated, victorious communist parties established their own model of party–military relations. In Singapore, the PAP took inspiration from Israel, whereas Siam had already developed a hierarchical military modeled after European examples well before World War I.

The different contexts in which postcolonial armies came about and their role in achieving independence and in defending new states against armed insurgencies had a strong impact on the subsequent development of civil–military relations. Legacies of colonial rule and the Japanese occupation created path dependencies that structured the shape of civil–military relations in the immediate postwar period. If independence came through revolutionary struggle and civilians had to rely heavily on the military's coercive and organizational means for achieving state sovereignty and ensuring their hold on power, the officer corps became a major source of political power and administrative capability. In this scenario, armies acted as transmitters of nationalism, diffusing national ideologies and anticolonialism among the populace at critical junctures, and became agents in the early creation of large-scale sociopolitical organizations (Lebra 1977: 3). In contrast, the future political influence of soldiers would be weaker when the processes of decolonialization was relatively orderly, and the military was not involved in putting down class-based or ethnic insurgencies.

However, the structure of the political party environment and of relations within the civilian elite during the formative years of civil–military relations mattered as well (see Table 7). Weak political organizations and a fractured elite structure characterized by ideological conflicts, mutual distrust, and unstable political regimes generated conditions of discordance that led to civil–military partnerships or military control (i.e., South Vietnam, Indonesia, Burma, Royalist Laos, and Thailand). In contrast, political systems with well-institutionalized political parties and ideologically or "consensually unified monocratic elites" (Burton, Gunther, and Higley 1992) such as Singapore, North Vietnam, and Malaysia, elite consensus and the organizational machinery of the ruling party generated conditions of concordance and convergence that resulted in stable and effective party control (Alagappa 2001a; Slater 2010b). Although political parties in the first Filipino democracy were institutionally weak (Landé 1965), a pluralistic political elite with the widely shared consensus to keep the military away from government had emerged during the colonial period. Yet, under President Marcos, the steadying effect of a unified elite structure diminished, with the initial conditions for civilian supremacy turning into conditions for a civil–military authoritarian partnership. The failure to institutionalize a strong political party increased the dictator's

Table 7 Formative Political Contexts of Southeast Asian Civil–Military Relations from the 1940s to the 1960s

Country	Peaceful achievement of independence	Class-based insurgencies	Communal insurgencies	Political parties/ civilian elite structure	Type of civil–military relations
Burma	Yes	Yes	Yes	Weak/ disunified	Praetorian
Cambodia	Yes	Yes	No	Weak/ disunified	Neopatrimonial
Indonesia	No	Yes	Yes	Weak/ disunified	Praetorian
Laos	Yes	Yes	No	Weak/ disunified	Praetorian
Malaysia	Yes	Yes	Yes	Strong/unified	Professional
North Vietnam	No	Yes	No	Strong/unified	Revolutionary
Philippines	Yes	Yes	No	Weak/unified	Professional (pre-1972)
South Vietnam	No	Yes	No	Weal/ disunified	Praetorian
Singapore	Yes	No	No	Strong/unified	Professional
Thailand	–	No	No	Weak/ disunified	Praetorian

vulnerable to elite defections, allowed opposition activists to develop unofficial networks to challenge regime domination, and forced the dictator to increasingly rely on the factionalized AFP.

5.2 Military Roles

Section 4 revealed a number of important similarities and differences among the main roles of Southeast Asian militaries. First, and most important, most militaries have traditionally been counterinsurgency forces, with their main mission being internal security, later redefined in anticommunist nations such as Thailand and the Philippines as "national security" because the enemy included subversive elements.

Second, compulsory military service not only has been a useful instrument for the relatively cheap and cost-efficient recruitment of soldiers for army-tilted militaries but also has been of crucial importance for processes of nation-building as well as in developing a common national identity across ethnic boundaries. Universal military conscription, if enforced, helped to make the armed forces ethnically more representative in their composition, if not leadership. In addition, compulsory military service has strong ideological underpinnings in the socialist countries and is a key instrument of political indoctrination aimed at inculcating recruits with socialist worldviews that would enable them to accept Party positions and the vanguard role of the Communist Party.

Third, in many countries the military played a key role in the exercise of political domination, either as ruler or through supporting nondemocratic and democratic governments. Although the region witnessed a number of mass protests that aimed at democratic regime change, there is no uniform pattern of military reactions to nonviolent mass mobilizations. In Indonesia and the Philippines, military elites refused to defend the dictator against the unarmed protesters, whereas in Myanmar and Thailand, military leaders decided to defend the autocratic government against the masses on the streets. However, not only do militaries' responses vary, but the consequences of military reactions to nonviolent mass protests also display some degree of variation in terms of actual regime changes. In the Philippines and Indonesia, military defection was crucial for democratic transition. In Indonesia, some military hardliners advocated cracking down on the protests, but the leadership decided to join civilian regime elites who defected from the dictator. This doomed Suharto's autocratic rule but probably saved the regime party, Golkar, from collapse and enabled the military leadership to play a highly influential role in the transition from authoritarian to democratic government, dominate the course and content of military reforms, and maintain its economic and political interests. In contrast, when in Burma the pseudocivilian regime party collapsed in the face of widespread social protests in 1988, military hardliners employed extreme measures to disperse the protest movement and restore direct military rule. In Thailand, mass protests in Bangkok in 1973 and 1992 were also met with military repression. In contrast to Burma, however, military strongmen were forced to step down despite military support when the royal palace intervened.

Fourth, Singapore and Malaysia, together with Brunei, are the only non-democratic regimes in the region in which the military has no relevant role in guaranteeing regime security or domestic stability or promoting economic development. In all other autocracies, soldiers have traditionally assumed vital roles in political domination, regime security, and/or modernizing the national economy.

Finally, the economic function is especially important in countries that have a long history of military or military strongman rule and in the socialist regimes of Laos and Vietnam. Section 4 demonstrated that military businesses often play a double role as pillars of promoting economic development and modernization, on the one hand, and providing patronage for the officer corps, on the other. However, only in some countries did military-owned enterprises become an important source of extrabudgetary revenue for the military establishment.

What drove the rise of military entrepreneurship in Southeast Asia was a complex combination of three sets of material, ideological, and political factors (see Table 8). The Burmese military had played an important role in the national economy since the 1950s and, especially, after Ne Win's turn to socialism in 1962. However, following the restoration of a direct military government in 1988, military entrepreneurs became the dominant actors in the emerging capitalist order. The nationalization of larger commercial and manufacturing establishments, including those of Indian traders, by the military government after 1962 removed the class of Indian–Burmese and Sino–Burmese capitalists who had dominated Burma's national economy since the British period. Unlike in Burma, military entrepreneurs in Thailand and Indonesia forged economic coalitions with local capitalists, often ethnic Chinese, whose economic strength contrasted with the vulnerabilities of a marginalized and threatened minority group (Sidel 2008).

In contrast, militaries in other Southeast Asian countries lacked the kind of structural, political, and cultural factors that motivated and enabled militaries of the first and second clusters to become businessmen and entrepreneurs. Neither the Chinese business communities in Singapore, Brunei, and Malaysia nor ethnic Chinese capitalists in the Philippines needed political protection from the military; either they were already the dominant ethnic

Table 8 Drivers of Military Entrepreneurship in Southeast Asia

Country	Critical economic juncture	Military's strategic-ideological justification	Coalitional opportunities
Myanmar	1988	Stabilizing military dominance	Ceasefire capitalists, foreign capital
Indonesia	1957	*Dwifungsi*	Sino-Indonesian capitalists, Golkar, Suharto family
Laos	1985	New economic measures	Party capitalists, foreign capital
Vietnam	1986	*doi moi*	Party cadres, foreign capital
Thailand	1957	Anticommunism	Sino-Thai capitalists foreign capital, US aid, and Crown Property Bureau

group, enjoying the protection of the monarchy, or their interests were sufficiently well represented by the existing political parties. For example, Malaysian Chinese businesses were well connected to the government through the Malaysian Chinese Association, one of the component parties of the ruling Alliance/Barisan Nasional that was in power from 1957. Moreover, the "Bargain" of 1955 provided Indians and Chinese with full citizenship and secure property rights under a capitalist system in return for the acceptance of Malay political supremacy over the other ethnic communities (Crouch 1996). Finally, the rise of military entrepreneurs in Vietnam and Laos is a consequence of the policies of economic transformation of the Communist Parties. Yet it contains potential for conflict between the Party and the military, especially in Vietnam, where military modernization has been driven by the external threat posed by China over territory in the contested South China Sea, while, at the same time, commercial activities threaten to diminish overall military preparedness and effectiveness.

5.3 Types of Civil–Military Relations

As reflected in Section 3, civil–military relations in Southeast Asia have undergone substantial changes over the last decades, but there have been significant continuities as well. Three broad findings need to be emphasized.

First, party regimes – single-party dictatorships in Laos and Vietnam and dominant-party systems in Malaysia and Singapore – exhibit highly stable civil–military relations. Unlike in cases such as Indonesia under Suharto, Burma under Ne Win, and Thailand from 1932 to 1992, where military strongmen organized their own political parties as tools for elite co-optation, elite bargaining, and building mass support, political parties came first in these states and created their national armed forces. Malaysia and Singapore maintained their professional militaries and strict civilian control under resilient authoritarian regimes. Communist Parties in Laos and Vietnam institutionalized supremacy over their armies and successfully maintained their ability to simultaneously minimize threats from the masses (i.e., mass protests) and from military elites. This stability contrasts with the trajectories of military and political regimes under military strongman rule.

Second, transitions from military-led autocracy to a political democracy actually involve two transitions. The first transition, if successful, is one from autocratic rule to the installation of a democratic government. Once a transition from authoritarian rule in a given country has reached this point, a second transition can begin. This second shift is from democratic government toward the effective functioning of a democratic regime or, in other words, to the consolidation of democracy (O'Donnell 1992). The challenge for democratic reformers during the first transition from military to civilian government is to achieve the inauguration of a democratic government without provoking military resistance. The challenge for democratic governments during the second transition toward an effective democratic regime is to establish democratic governance of civil–military relations. This challenge is especially acute and arduous in countries where the military was able to carve out substantial political roles or took over the government shortly after the country's independence or emergence as a modern nation-state and where it preserved such privileges during the first transition. This has been especially true for Indonesia, Thailand, and Myanmar. In these three countries, a military government either dictated the transition (Thailand and Myanmar) or, at least, was able to negotiate the terms of its retreat from the center of the political stage (Indonesia).

Why did civilian politicians in Southeast Asia consent to military tutelage that restricted the possible range of democratic outcomes, thereby introducing a source of instability into the political system? One reason is that moderate civilian reformists feared that any attempt to impose civilian control would have immediately provoked exactly what it intended to eliminate – military intervention (Croissant 2015). A second reason is that in countries with a long tradition of military intervention – such as Thailand, Myanmar, and

Indonesia – institutional models through which civilians could have exercised control over the military were absent at the time of the transition from military to civilian government. Third, the issue of civilian control over the military is not only whether it is prudent to attempt it but also who wants to have it. In this regard, the case of Thailand is telling. In post-2006 Thailand, anti-Thaksin political forces simply preferred military tutelage and autonomy as a protection from popular mobilization and from demands for greater political participation and economic redistribution.

Finally, it is worth highlighting that just as democratization is neither a necessary nor a sufficient condition for the establishment of civilian control over the military, changes in political–military relations can also take place without an outright transition of the political regime. For example, in Vietnam, profound economic reforms pressured governments to adjust the foundations for greater institutionalization, which went hand-in-hand with changes in the military's organization and roles and a recalibration of civil–military relations. At the same time, the revolution in military affairs and rapidly changing threat assessments promote professional military education and the modernization of military organizations. Similar to Laos and other Communist Party regimes in their maturation phase, the Vietnamese military's relation with the Party has evolved from a "symbiotic" one into a "coalitional" one (Perlmutter and LeoGrande 1982: 782). Although the Lao and Vietnam Communist Parties continue to direct and supervise all other state institutions, including the military, their political supremacy is necessarily limited by the division of labor among various institutions. There is usually little conflict between Party and army; on issues of "normal politics," the military acts as a functionally specific elite engaged in bargaining to defend its perceived institutional interests; and in crisis politics, the military is a political resource that various Party factions seek to enlist against their opponents.

5.4 *Quo Vadis* Civil– Military Relations?

Ultimately, when assessing the development of civil–military relations in the region from independence into the early twenty-first century, it seems evident that the political role of the military has seen significant changes *and* continuities. Conventional indicators such as the number of military regimes and the frequency of military coups and attempted coups seem to indicate a declining political role of soldiers in Southeast Asia. Similarly, there has been a decline in the number of countries under military rule, from the peak in 1971, when six of ten states were ruled by military officers, to only one in 2018. This is mainly the result of two developments. First, the collapse of military-led anticommunist regimes in Indochina in 1975 and, second, Indonesia's transition from military strongman rule to democracy and the transformation of direct military rule into multiparty authoritarianism with military tutelage in Myanmar. The Thai case seems to belie these developments because the country is currently under the strictest form of military rule since the mid-1970s. However, Thailand is not the avant-garde of a resurgent political role of the military in Southeast Asia but an anachronism. Despite recurring pledges to hold national-level elections since the 2014 coup, junta leader and Prime Minister General (ret.) Prayuth Chan-ocha has made it clear that the military plans to remain in power for the foreseeable future, providing political cover for the established monarchic–military symbiotic order, most probably through the restoration of a military-guided multiparty system. However, in contrast to Myanmar, where an uncontested and cohesive Tatmadaw initiated and controlled the transition from direct military rule to a civilian government, the Thai junta's reluctance to follow the example of previous military rulers is an indicator of the underlying weakness of the military as a guardian of monarchical power. On the one hand, the generals could possibly govern without multiparty elections and an elected parliament, although the resulting legitimacy deficit would in the long run require a much greater use of force and coercion. On the other hand, the military has good reason to be fearful of "the specter of a post-election return to power by the Shinawatra dynasty" (McCargo 2018: 184). It is hard to see how the military government can find a way out of this dilemma.

Although the possibility of a military coup may seem increasingly remote in most countries of Southeast Asia, except perhaps Thailand and Myanmar, and the regional wave of democratization opened critical windows of opportunity for civilians to realign civil–military relations, it is important to reiterate that democratic reform processes in Southeast Asia did *not* create democratic civil–military relations in which the armed forces are fully under political control of democratically legitimized authorities. Furthermore, there is no indication of any erosion of established practices of political control over the military in Singapore, Malaysia,[14] Laos, and Vietnam or in other unambiguously authoritarian regimes such as Brunei and Cambodia. Given the fact that

---

[14] It is unlikely that the change of government in Malaysia in May 2018 will negatively affect civil–military relations. After all, the new ruling coalition (*Harapan Pakatan* ["Alliance of Hope"]) of Premier Minister Mahathir Mohamad, a former Prime Minister under the Barisan Nasional (BN) government, is a multiethnic party coalition, and it seems inconceivable that the new government will adopt a policy that would change the preferential treatment of the majority Malay community and other indigenous peoples in the armed forces. Moreover, if the main argument of this study is correct, the legacies of six decades of civilian control over the military in Malaysia should be strong enough to survive the government turnover, especially because Mahathir's People's Justice Party is to a large extent a breakaway faction of the UMNO/BN.

much of the academic literature implicitly equates civilian control of the military with democracy, it is ironic that at the beginning of the twenty-first century the factor of military tutelary powers is more often a problem in political regimes with a democratically elected government than in regimes that have a nondemocratic government but a strong ruling party. In contrast, this might offer a silver lining for those in Southeast Asia and in the West who hope for future democratic changes in the region: there are certainly many obstacles for future democratization in the authoritarian regimes of the region. With the exception of Myanmar and Thailand, however, civil–military relations and military praetorianism are not one of them.

References

Abul-Magd, Zeinab (2017). *Militarizing the Nation: The Army, Business, and Revolution in Egypt.* New York, NY: Columbia University Press.

Abuza, Zachary, and Nguyen Nhat Anh (2016). "Little fallout: Vietnam's security policy after the 12th Congress of the Vietnam Communist Party," Center for International Maritime Security. Available at http://cimsec.org/21720–2/21720 (accessed June 2, 2017).

Agüero, Felipe (1998). "Legacies of transitions: institutionalization, the military, and democracy in South America," *Mershon International Studies Review* 42:383–404.

Ahmad, Abu Taljib (2009). "The impact of Japanese occupation on colonial and anti-colonial armies in Southeast Asia," in *Colonial Armies in Southeast Asia*, ed. Karl Hack and Tobias Rettig. London: Routledge, 213–38.

Ahmad, Zakaria Haji (1988). "The military and development in Malaysia and Brunei, with a short survey on Singapore," in *Soldiers and Stability in Southeast Asia*, ed. J. Soedjati Djiwandono and Yong Mun Cheong. Singapore: ISEAS, 231–54.

Alagappa, Muthiah (1988). "Military professionalism and the development role of the military in Southeast Asia," in *Soldiers and Stability in Southeast Asia*, ed. J. Soedjati Djiwandono and Yong Mun Cheong. Singapore: ISEAS, 15–48.

Alagappa, Muthiah (2001a). "Conclusion," in *Coercion and Governance: The Declining Political Role of the Military in Asia*, ed. Muthiah Alagappa. Stanford, CA: Stanford University Press, 433–98.

Alagappa, Muthiah (2001b). "Introduction," in *Coercion and Governance: The Declining Political Role of the Military in Asia*, ed. Muthiah Alagappa. Stanford, CA: Stanford University Press, 1–28.

Aminuddin, M. Faishal (2017). "The Purnawirawan and party development in post-authoritarian Indonesia, 1998–2014," *Journal of Current Southeast Asian Affairs* 36:3–30.

Aphornsuvan, Thanet (2001). *The Search for Order: Constitutions and Human Rights in Thai Political History.* Available at https://openresearch-repository.anu.edu.au/bitstream/1885/42075/2/Thanet.pdf (accessed August 3, 2018).

Aspinall, Edward (2005). *Opposing Suharto: Compromise, Resistance, and Regime Change in Indonesia.* Stanford, CA: Stanford University Press.

Baird, Ian (2010). *Quotas, Powers, Patronage and Illegal Rent Seeking: The Political Economy of Logging and the Timber Trade in Southern Laos.* Washington, DC: Forest Trends.

Barany, Zoltan (2012). *The Soldier and the Changing State: Building Democratic Armies in Africa, Asia, Europe, and the Americas*. Princeton, NJ: Princeton University Press.

Barr, Michael D. (2014). *The Ruling Elite of Singapore: Networks of Power and Influence*. London: I.B. Tauris

Beeson, Mark, and Alex J. Bellamy (2008). *Securing Southeast Asia: The Politics of Security Sector Reform*. London: Routledge.

Brömmelhörster, Jörn, and Wolf-Christian Paes (2003). "Soldiers in business: an introduction," in *The Military As an Economic Actor: Soldiers in Business*, ed. Jörn Brömmelhörster and Wolf-Christian Paes. Basingstoke: Palgrave, 1–18.

Brown, Cameron S., Christopher J. Fariss, and R. Blake McMahon (2016). "Recouping after coup-proofing: compromised military effectiveness and strategic substitution," *International Interactions* 42:1–30.

Brown, Rajeswary Ampalavanar (2006). "Indonesian corporations, cronyism, and corruption," *Modern Asian Studies* 40: 953–92.

Bünte, Marco (2017). "The NLD–military coalition in Myanmar: military guardianship and its economic foundations," in *Khaki Capital: The Political Economy of the Military in Southeast Asia*, ed. Paul W. Chambers and Napisa Waitoolkiat. Copenhagen: NIAS, 93–129.

Bureau of Arms Control, Verification, and Compliance (2017). *World Military Expenditures and Arms Transfers 1998–2016*, US Department of State. Available at www.state.gov/t/avc/rls/rpt/wmeat/.

Burton, Michael, Richard Gunther, and John Higley (1992). *Elites and Democratic Consolidation in Latin America and Southern Europe*. Cambridge: Cambridge University Press.

Callahan, Mary P. (2005). *Making Enemies: War and State Building in Burma*. Ithaca, NY: Cornell University Press.

Case, William (2002). *Politics in Southeast Asia: Democracy or Less*. Richmond, VA: Curzon Press.

Case, William (2015). "Democracy's mixed fortunes in Southeast Asia: Topor, change, and trade-offs," in *Routledge Handbook of Southeast Asian Democratization*, ed. William Case. London: Routledge, 3–23.

Celoza, Albert F. (1997). *Ferdinand Marcos and the Philippines: The Political Economy of Authoritarianism*. New York, NY: Praeger.

Central Intelligence Agency (CIA) (2017). *CIA World Factbook*. Available at www.cia.gov/library/publications/the-world-factbook/.

Chambers, Paul W. (2010). "Thailand on the brink: resurgent military, eroded democracy," *Asian Survey* 50: 835–58.

Chambers, Paul W. (2013). *Knights of the Realm: Thailand's Military and Policy Then and Now*. Bangkok: White Lotus Press.

Chambers, Paul. W. (2015). "'Neo-Sultanistic Tendencies:' The Trajectory of Civil-Military Relations in Cambodia", *Asian Security* 11: 179–205.

Chambers, Paul W. (2017). "Khaki clientelism: the political economy of Cambodia's security forces," in *Khaki Capital: The Political Economy of the Military in Southeast Asia*, ed. Paul W. Chambers and Napisa Waitoolkiat. Copenhagen: NIAS, 161–217.

Chambers, Paul W., and Napisa Waitoolkiat 2016. "The resilience of monarchised military in Thailand," *Journal of Contemporary Asia* 46: 425–44.

Chambers, Paul W., and Napisa Waitoolkiat (2017). "Arch-royalist rent: the political economy of the military in Thailand," in *Khaki Capital: The Political Economy of the Military in Southeast Asia*, ed. Paul W. Chambers and Napisa Waitoolkiat. Copenhagen: NIAS, 40–92.

Chong, Alan, and Samuel Chan (2017). "Militarizing civilians in Singapore: preparing for 'crisis' within a calibrated nationalism," *Pacific Review* 30: 365–84.

Connors, Michael K. (2003). *Democracy and National Identity in Thailand*. New York, NY: Routledge.

Croissant, Aurel (2008). "The perils and promises of democratization through United Nations transitional authority: lessons from Cambodia and East Timor, *Democratization* 15: 649–68.

Croissant, Aurel (2015). "Southeast Asian militaries in the age of democratization: from ruler to servant?," in *Routledge Handbook of Southeast Asian Democratization*, ed. William Case. London: Routledge, 314–32.

Croissant, Aurel (2016). "Civil-military relations in Asia," in Oxford Bibliographies in Political Science, ed. Sandy Maisel. New York, NY: Oxford University Press.

Croissant, Aurel, and Tanja Eschenauer (2018). "The Military and Politics in North Africa and the Levant," in *Routledge Handbook of Mediterranean Politics*, ed. Richard Gillespie and Frederic Volpi. New York and London: Routledge, 157–170.

Croissant, Aurel, and Jil Kamerling (2013). "Why do military regimes institutionalize? Constitution-making and elections as political survival strategy in Myanmar," *Asian Journal of Political Science* 21: 105–25.

Croissant, Aurel, and Jil Kamerling (2013). "Why do military regimes institutionalize? Constitution-making and elections as political survival strategy in Myanmar," *Asian Journal of Political Science* 21: 105–25.

Croissant, Aurel, and David Kuehn (2015). "The military's role in politics," in *Routledge Handbook of Comparative Political Institutions*, ed Jennifer Gandhi and Ruben Ruiz-Rufino. London: Routledge, 258–77.

Croissant, Aurel, and David Kuehn (2018). "Military and politics," in *Routledge Handbook of Asian Politics*, ed. Shiping Hua. New York, NY: Routledge, 413–29.

Croissant, Aurel, and Philip Lorenz (2018). *Comparative Politics of Southeast Asia: An Introduction to Governments and Political Regimes*. Heidelberg: Springer.

Croissant, Aurel, Tanja Eschenauer, and Jil Kamerling (2017). "Militaries' roles in political regimes: introducing the PRM data set," *European Political Science* 16: 400–14.

Croissant, Aurel, David Kuehn, Philip Lorenz, and Paul W. Chambers (2013). *Civilian Control and Democracy in Asia*, Basingstoke: Palgrave.

Crouch, Harold (1978). *The Army and Politics in Indonesia*. Ithaca, NY: Cornell University Press.

Crouch, Harold (1991). "The military in Malaysia," in *The Military, the State, and Development in Asia and the Pacific*, ed. V. Selochan, Boulder, CO: Westview Press, 121–37.

Crouch, Harold (1996). *Government and Society in Malaysia*. Ithaca, NY: Cornell University Press.

Dwyer, Michael B. (2014). "Micro-geopolitics: capitalising security in Laos's Golden Quadrangle," *Geopolitics* 19:377–405.

Dwyer, Michael B., Micah L. Ingalls, and Ian G. Baird (2016). "The security exception: development and militarization in Laos's protected areas," *Geoforum* 69: 207–17.

Edmonds, Martin (1988). *Armed Services and Society*. Leicester: Leicester University Press.

Edmunds, Timothy M. (2012). "Security sector reform," in *Routledge Handbook of Civil-Military Relations*, ed. Thomas C. Bruneau and Florina Cristiana Matei. London: Routledge.

Egreteau, Renaud (2017). "Embedding praetorianism: soldiers, state, and constitutions in postcolonial Myanmar," in *Politics and Constitutions in Southeast Asia*, ed. Marco Bünte and Björn Dressel. New York, NY: Routledge, 117–39.

Feaver, Peter D. (1999). "Civil-military relations," *Annual Review of Political Science* 2: 211–41.

Feijó, Rui Gracia (2018). "Timor-Leste in 2017: between a diplomatic victory and the return of 'belligerent democracy,'" *Asian Survey* 58: 206–12.

Feith, Herbert (1962). *The Decline of Constitutional Democracy in Indonesia*. Ithaca, NY: Cornell University Press.

Ferrara, Federico (2003). "Why regimes create disorder: Hobbes's dilemma during a Rangoon summer," *Journal of Conflict Resolution* 47: 302–25.

Fink, Christina (2009). *Living Silence: Burma under Military Rule* (2nd edn). Bangkok: Silkworm Press.

Fink, Christina (2018). "Myanmar in 2017: insecurity and violence," *Asian Survey* 58: 158–75.

Funston, N. John (2006). "Thailand: reform politics," In *Government and Politics in Southeast Asia*, ed. N. John Funston. Singapore: ISEAS, 328–71.

Geddes, Barbara (2003). *Paradigms and Sand Castles: Theory Building and Research Design in Comparative Politics*. Ann Arbor, MI: University of Michigan Press.

Geddes, Barbara, Joseph Wright, and Erica Frantz (2014). "Military rule," *Annual Review of Political Science* 17: 147–62.

Grewert, Elke, and Zeinab Abul-Magd (eds.) (2016). *Businessmen in Arms: How the Military and Other Armed Groups Profit in the MENA Region*. London: Rowman & Littlefield.

Gunawan, Aditya B. (2017). "Civilian control and defense policy in Indonesia's nascent democracy," In *Reforming Civil-Military Relations in New Democracies*, ed. Aurel Croissant and David Kuehn. Heidelberg: Springer, 129–50.

Guyot, Dorothy (1966). "The Burma Independence Army: a political movement in military garb," in *Southeast Asia in World War II: Four Essays*, ed. Joseph Silverstein. New Haven, CT: Yale University Press, 51–65.

Hack, Karl (2009). "Imperialism and decolonization in Southeast Asia: colonial forces and British world power," in *Colonial Armies in Southeast Asia*, ed. Karl Hack and Tobias Rettig, London: Routledge, 239–66.

Hack, Karl, and Tobias Rettig (2009a). "Imperial systems of power, colonial forces and the making of modern Southeast Asia," in *Colonial Armies in Southeast Asia*, ed. Karl Hack and Tobias Rettig. London: Routledge, 3–38.

Hack, Karl, and Tobias Rettig (2009b). "Demography and domination in Southeast Asia," in *Colonial Armies in Southeast Asia*, ed. Karl Hack and Tobias Rettig. London: Routledge, 39–73.

Hall, Rosalie Arcala (2017). "Philippine military capital after 1986: norming, holdouts and new frontiers," in *Khaki Capital: The Political Economy of the Military in Southeast Asia*, ed. Paul W. Chambers and Napisa Waitoolkiat. Copenhagen: NIAS. 271–305.

Handley, Paul M. (2006). *The King Never Smiles: A Biography of Thailand's Bhumibol Adulyadej*. New Haven, CT: Yale University Press.

Hanson, Victor David (2017). *The Second World Wars: How the First Global Conflict Was Fought and Won*. New York, NY: Basic Books.

Hedman, Eva-Lotta (2001). "The Philippines: not so military, not so civil," in *Coercion and Governance: The Declining Political Role of the Military in Asia*, ed. Muthiah Alagappa. Stanford, CA: Stanford University Press, 165–86.

Hernandez, Carolina G. (1985). "The Philippine military and civilian control: under Marcos and beyond," *Third World Quarterly* 7: 907–23.

Hernandez, Carolina G. (2006). "The military in Philippine politics: democratization, governance, and security sector reform," in *Philippine Politics and Governance: Challenges to Democratization and Development*, ed. T. S. E. Tadem and N. M. Morada. Diliman: University of the Philippines Press, 391–408.

Hernandez, K. M. G., and H. J. S. Kraft (2010). "Armed forces as veto power: civil-military relations in the Philippines," in *Democracy under Stress: Civil-Military Relations in South and Southeast Asia*, ed. Paul W. Chambers and Aurel Croissant. Bangkok: ISIS, 126–48.

Hewison, Kevin, and Kengkij Kitirianglarp (2010). "Thai-style democracy: the royalist struggle for Thailand's politics," in *Saying the Unsayable: Monarchy and Democracy in Thailand*, ed. S. Ivarsson and L. Isager. Copenhagen: NIAS Press, 179–203.

Hoadley, John S. (1975). *Soldiers and Politics in Souteast Asia: Civil-Military Relations in Comparative Perspective, 1933–1975* (reprint 2012). New Brunswick, NJ: Transaction Books.

Hodgdon, Benjamin D. (2008). "Frontier country: the political culture of logging and development on the periphery in Laos," *Kyoto Journal* 69:58–65.

Honna, Jun (2017). "The politics of securing khaki capitalism in democratizing Indonesia," in *Khaki Capital: The Political Economy of the Military in Southeast Asia*, ed. Paul W. Chambers and Napisa Waitoolkiat, Copenhagen: NIAS. 305–27.

Horner, Layton (1973). *Japanese Military Administration in Malaya and the Philippines*. The University of Arizona, ProQuest Dissertations Publishing.

Huxley, Tim (2000). *Defending the Lion City: The Armed Forces of Singapore*. St. Leonards: Allen & Unwin.

International Institute for Strategic Studies (IISS) (2017). *The Military Balance, 2017*. London: Oxford University Press.

Kammen, Damien (2013). "The armed forces in Timor-Leste: politicization through elite conflict," in *The Political Resurgence of the Military in Southeast Asia: Conflict and Leadership*, ed. Marcus Mietzner. New York, NY: Routledge, 107–26.

Kessler, Richard J. (1989). *Rebellion and Repression in the Philippines*. New Haven, CT: Yale University Press.

Kim, Insoo (2008). *Bringing the Military Back in Political Transition: Democratic Transition by and for Powerless Officers in South Korea.* Madison, WI: UMI Dissertation Publishing.

Koehler, Kevin (2016). "Officers and regimes: the historical origins of political military-relations in the Middle East and North Africa," in *Armies and Insurgencies in the Arab Spring*, ed. Holger Albrecht, Aurel Croissant, and Fred H. Lawson. Philadelphia, PA: University of Pennsylvania Press, 34–53.

Kraisoraphong, Keokam (2014). "Crossing the threshold: Thailand's path to rethinking security sector governance," In *Peacebuilding and Security Sector Governance in Asia*, ed. Yuji Uesugi. Zürich: LIT Verlag, 77–104.

Laksmana, Evan A. (2008). "Spoilers, partners, and pawns: military organizational behaviour and civil-military relations in Indonesia," RSIS Working Paper No. 161, S. Rajaratnam School of International Studies, Singapore.

Lall, Marie (2016). *Understanding Reform in Myanmar: People and Society in the Wake of Military Rule.* London: Hurst.

Landé, Carl H. (1965). *Leaders, Factions, and Parties: The Structure of Philippine Politics.* New Haven, CT: Yale University Press.

Lebra, Joyce C. (1977). *Japanese-Trained Armies in Southeast Asia: Independence and Volunteer Forces in World War II.* Hong Kong: Heinemann Educational Books.

Lee, Eun Ho (1971). *The Role of the Military in Nation-Building: A Comparative Study of South Vietnam and South Korea.* Southern Illinois University at Carbondale: ProQuest Dissertations and Theses.

Lee, Terence (2009). "The armed forces and transitions from authoritarian rule: explaining the role of the military in 1986 Philippines and 1998 Indonesia," *Comparative Political Studies* 42: 640–69.

Lee, Terence (2015). *Defect or Defend. Military Responses to Popular Protests in Authoritarian Asia.* Baltimore, MD: Johns Hopkins University Press.

Lipp, Hans, and Paul Chambers (2017). "Earning their keep: the political economy of the military in Laos," in *Khaki Capital: The Political Economy of the Military in Southeast Asia*, ed. Paul Chambers and Napisa Waitoolkiat. Copenhagen: NIAS, 218–70.

Lissak, Moshe (1976). *Military Roles in Modernization: Civil-Military Relations in Thailand and Burma.* Beverly Hills, CA: Sage Publications.

LoGorfo, James P. (1997). *Civil Society and Democratization in Thailand, 1973–1992.* New York, NY: ProQuest Dissertations and Theses.

Mahoney, James, and Dietrich Rueschemeyer (2003). "Comparative historical analysis: achievements and agendas," in *Comparative Historical Analysis in the Social Sciences*, ed. James Mahoney and Dietrich Rueschemeyer, Cambridge: Cambridge University Press, 3–40.

Mani, Kristina (2011). "Militares empresarios: approaches to studying the military as an economic actor," *Bulletin of Latin American Research* 30: 183–97.

Maung, Aung Myoe (2007). "A historical overview of political transition in Myanmar since 1988," Asia Research Institute Working Paper Series No. 95, NUS, Singapore.

McCargo, Duncan (2005). "Network monarchy and legitimacy crises in Thailand," *Pacific Review* 18:499–519.

McCargo, Duncan (2018). "Thailand in 2017: politics on hold," *Asian Survey* 58: 181–87.

McCargo, Duncan, and Pathmanand Ukrist (2005). *The Thaksinization of Thailand*. Copenhagen: NIAS.

McCulloch, Lesley (2003). "Trifungsi: the role of the Indonesian military in business," in *The Military As an Economic Actor: Soldiers in Business*, ed. Jörn Brömmelhörster and Wolf-Christian Paes. Basingstoke: Palgrave, 94–123.

McLeod, R. H. (2008). "Inadequate budgets and salaries as instruments for institutionalizing public sector corruption in Indonesia," *South East Asia Research* 16:199–223.

Meixsel, Richard (2009). "American exceptionalism in colonial forces? The Philippine Scout mutiny of 1924," in *Colonial Armies in Southeast Asia*, ed. Karl Hack and Tobias Rettig. London: Routledge, 171–93.

Mérieau, Eugenie (2017). "The legal-military alliance for illiberal constitutionalism in Thailand," in *Politics and Constitutions in Southeast Asia*, ed. Marco Bünte and Björn Dressel. New York, NY: Routledge, 140–61.

Mietzner, Marcus (2009). *Military Politics, Islam, and the State in Indonesia: From Turbulent Transition to Democratic Consolidation*. Singapore: ISEAS.

Mietzner, Marcus (2011). "Conflict and leadership: the resurgent political role of the military in Southeast Asia," in *The Political Resurgence of the Military in Southeast Asia: Conflict and Leadership*, ed. Marcus Mietzner. London: Routledge, 1–23.

Mietzner, Marcus (2017). "Stateness and state capacity in post-authoritarian Indonesia: securing democracy's survival, entrenching its low quality," unpublished manuscript.

Mietzner, Marcus (2018). "The Indonesian armed forces, coalitional presidentialism, and democratization," in *Routledge Handbook of Contemporary Indonesia*, ed. Robert Hefner. London: Routledge, 140–51.

Mietzner, Marcus, and L. Misol (2012). "Military businesses in post-Suharto Indonesia: decline, reform and persistence," in *The Politics of Military*

Reform: Experiences from Indonesia and Nigeria, ed. J. Rüland, M. G. Manea, and H. Born. Heidelberg: Springer, 101–22.

Min, Win (2008). "Looking inside the Burmese military," *Asian Survey* 48: 1018–37.

Miranda, Felipe B., and Ruben F. Ciron (1988). "Development and the military in the Philippines: military perceptions in a time of continuing crisis," In *Soldiers and Stability in Southeast Asia*, ed. J. Soedjati Djiwandono and Yong Mun Cheong. Singapore: ISEAS, 163–212.

Montiel, Cristina Jayme (2010). "Social representations of democratic transition: was the Philippine People Power a non-violent power shift or a military coup?," *Asian Journal of Social Psychology* 13: 173–84.

Morgenbesser, Lee (2017). "Misclassification on the Mekong: the origins of Hun Sen's personalist dictatorship," *Democratization* 25:192–208.

Myrttinen, Henri (2012). "Guerillas, gangsters, and contractors: reintegrating former combatants and its impact on SSR and development in post-conflict societies," In *Back to the Roots: Security Sector Reform and Development*, ed. A. Schnabel and V. Farr. Münster: LIT Verlag, 225–47.

Nathan, K. S., and Geetha Govindasamy (2001). "Malaysia: a congruence of interests," In *Coercion and Governance: The Declining Political Role of the Military in Asia*, ed. M. Alagappa. Stanford, CA: Stanford University Press, 259–75.

Ockey, James (2001). "Thailand: the struggle to redefine civil-military relations," In *Coercion and Governance: The Declining Political Role of the Military in Asia*, ed. Muthiah Alagappa. Stanford, CA: Stanford University Press, 187–209.

O'Donnell, Guillermo A. (1992). "Transitions, continuities, and paradoxes," in *Issues in Democratic Consolidation: The New South American Democracies in Comparative Perspective*, ed. Scott Mainwaring, Guillermo O'Donnell, and Samuel J. Valenzuela. Notre Dame, IN: University of Notre Dame Press, 17–52.

Osborne, Milton E. (1990). *Southeast Asia: An Illustrated History*. Ithaca, NY: Cornell University Press.

Pathmanand, Ukrist (2008). "A different coup d'état?," *Journal of Contemporary Asia* 38: 124–42.

Peled, Alon (1995). *Soldiers Apart: A Study in Ethnic Military Manpower Policies in Singapore, Israel, and South Africa*. Ann Arbor. MI: University of Michigan Press.

Perlmutter, Amos (1977). *The Military and Politics in Modern Times: On Professionals, Praetorians, and Ordinary Soldiers*. New Haven, CT: Yale University Press.

Perlmutter, Amos (1974). *Egypt, the Praetorian State*. New Brunswick, NJ: Transaction Publishers.

Perlmutter, Amos, and William M. LeoGrande (1982). "The party in uniform: toward a theory of civil-military relations in communist political systems," *American Political Science Review* 76: 778–89.

Pion-Berlin, David, and Rafael Martinez (2017). *Soldiers, Politicians, and Civilians: Reforming Civil-Military Relations in Democratic Latin America*. New York, NY: Oxford University Press.

Powell, Jonathan M., and Clayton L. Thyne. (2011). "Global instances of coups from 1950 to 2010," *Journal of Peace Research* 48: 249–59.

Prasirtsuk, Kitti (2015). "Thailand in 2014: another coup, a different coup?," *Asian Survey* 55: 200–6.

Rappa, Antonio L. (2017). *The King and the Making of Modern Thailand*. London: Routledge.

Raymond, Gregory Vincent (2017). "Naval modernization in Southeast Asia: under the shadow of army dominance?," *Contemporary Southeast Asia* 39: 149–77.

Richardson, Sophie, and Peter Sainsbury (2009). "Security sector reform in Cambodia," in *Security Sector Reform and Post-Conflict Peacebuilding*, ed. Albrecht Schnabel and Hans-Georg Ehrhart. Tokio: United Nations University Press, 283–96.

Ricklefs, Merle Calvin (2008). *A History of Modern Indonesia since c. 1200*. Basingstoke: Palgrave.

Riggs, Fred W. (1966). *Thailand: The Modernization of a Bureaucratic Polity*. Honolulu, HI: University of Hawaii Press.

Roosa, John (2007). "Finalising the nation: the Indonesian military as the guarantor of national unity," *Asia Pacific Viewpoint* 48:99–111.

Sahin, Selver B., and Donald Feaver (2013). "The politics of security sector reform in 'fragile' or 'post-conflict' settings: a critical review of the experience in Timor-Leste," *Democratization* 20: 1056–80.

Said, Salim (2006). *Legitimizing Military Rule: Indonesian Armed Forces Ideology, 1958–2000*. Jakarta: Pustaka Sinar Harapan.

Sarkees, Meredith Reid, and Frank Whelon Wayman (2010). *Resort to War: A Data Guide to Inter-State, Extra-State, Intra-State, and Non-State Wars, 1816–2007*. Washington, DC: CQ Press.

Samudavanija, Chai-anan (1971). *The Politics and Administration of the Thai Budgetary Process*. University of Wisconsin: ProQuest Dissertations and Theses.

Samudavanija, Chai-anan (1982). *The Thai Young Turks*. Singapore: ISEAS.

Samudavanija, Chai-anan (1989). "Thailand: A Stable Semidemocracy," in *Politics in Developing Countries: Comparing Experiences with Democracy*, ed. L. Diamond, J. J. Linz, and S. M. Lipset. Boulder and London: Lynne Rienner Publishers.

Searle, Peter (1999). *The Riddle of Malaysian Capitalism: Rent-Seekers or Real Capitalists?* Honolulu, HI: University of Hawaii Press.

Selth, Andrew (2002). *Burma's Armed Forces: Power without Glory*. Norwalk, CT: Eastbridge.

Shin, Doh-chul, and Rollin F. Tusalem (2009) "East Asia," in *Democratization*, ed. C. W. Haerpfer, P. Bernhagen, R. F. Inglehart, and C. Welzel. Oxford: Oxford University Press, 356–76.

Sidel, John T. (2008). "Social origins of dictatorship and democracy revisited: colonial state and Chinese immigrants in the making of modern Southeast Asia," *Comparative Politics* 40: 127–47.

Sirivunnabood, Punchada, and Jacob Ricks (2016). "Professionals and soldiers: measuring professionalism in the Thai military," *Pacific Affairs* 89:7–30.

Slater, Dan (2010a). "Altering authoritarianism: institutional complexity and autocratic agency in Indonesia," in *Explaining Institutional Change: Ambiguity, Agency, and Power*, ed. James Mahoney and Kathleen Thelen. New York, NY: Cambridge University Press, 132–67.

Slater, Dan (2010b). *Ordering Power: Contentious Politics and Authoritarian Leviathans in Southeast Asia*. Cambridge: Cambridge University Press.

Smith, Martin J. (1991). *Burma: Insurgency and the Politics of Ethnicity*. London: Zed Books.

Somvichian, Kamol (1969). *The Thai Military in Politics: An Analytical Study*. London: SOAS.

Steinberg, David I. (2001). *Burma, the State of Myanmar*. Washington, DC: Georgetown University Press.

Steinberg, David I. (2010). *Burma/Myanmar: What Everyone Needs to Know*. New York, NY: Oxford University Press.

Stockholm International Peace Research Institute (SIPRI) (2017). Military Expenditure Database, available at https://www.sipri.org (accessed August 3, 2018).

Stockwell, A. J. (1999). "Southeast Asia in war and peace: the end of European colonial empires," in *Cambridge History of Southeast Asia*, vol. II, part 2: *From World War II to the Present*, ed. Nicholas Tarling. New York, NY: Cambridge University Press, 1–58.

Stuart-Fox, Martin (2002). *Buddhist Kingdom, Marxist State: The Making of Modern Laos* (2nd edn). Bangkok: White Lotus Press.

Stuart-Fox, Martin (2006). *Laos – May 2006: The Eighth Congress of the Lao People's Revolutionary Party: More of the Same.* Available at www.aseanfocus.com/asiananalysis/article.cfm?articleID963.

Stuart-Fox, Martin (2009). "Laos: the Chinese connection," *Southeast Asian Affairs* 2009: 141–69.

Sundhausen, Ulf (1982). *The Road to Power: Indonesian Military Politics, 1945–1967.* New York, NY: Oxford University Press.

Svolik, Milan W. (2012). *The Politics of Authoritarian Rule.* Cambridge: Cambridge University Press.

Tamada, Yoshifumi (1995). "Coups in Thailand, 1980–1991: classmates, internal conflicts and relations with the government of the military," *Southeast Asian Studies* 33: 317–39.

Tan, Tai Yong (2001). "Singapore: civil-military fusion," In *Coercion and Governance: The Declining Political Role of the Military in Asia*, ed. Muthiah Alagappa. Stanford, CA: Stanford University Press, 276–93.

Tan, Tai Yong (2011). "The armed forces and politics in Singapore: the persistence of civil-military fusion," In *The Political Resurgence of the Military in Southeast Asia: Conflict and Leadership*, ed. Marcus Mietzner. New York, NY: Routledge, 148–67.

Taylor, Robert H. (1996). "Elections in Burma/Myanmar: for whom and why?," in *The Politics of Elections in Southeast Asia*, ed. Robert H. Taylor. Cambridge, MA: Woodrow Wilson Center Press, 164–83.

Thayer, Carlyle A. (2003). "The economic and commercial roles of the Vietnam People's Army," in *The Military as an Economic Actor: Soldiers in Business*, ed. Jörn Brömmelhörster and Wolf-Christian Paes. Basingstoke: Palgrave, 4–94.

Thayer, Carlyle A. (2013). "Military politics in contemporary Vietnam: political engagement, corporate interests, and professionalism," In *The Political Resurgence of the Military in Southeast Asia: Conflict and Leadership*, ed. Muthiah Mietzner. New York, NY: Routledge, 63–84.

Thayer, Carlyle A. (2017). "The political economy of military-run enterprises in Vietnam," in *Khaki Capital: The Political Economy of the Military in Southeast Asia*, ed. Paul W. Chambers and Napisa Waitoolkiat. Copenhagen: NIAS, 130–60.

Thompson, Mark R. (1995). *The Anti-Marcos Struggle: Personalistic Rule and Democratic Transition in the Philippines.* New Haven and London: Yale University Press.

Tigno, Jorge V. (2018). "The Philippines in 2017," *Asian Survey* 58: 142–48.

Tomsa, Dirk (2008). *Party Politics and Democratization in Indonesia: Golkar in the Post-Suharto Era.* New York, NY: Routledge.

Turley, William S. (1977). "Origins and development of communist military leadership in Vietnam," *Armed Forces and Society* 3: 219–43.

Var, Veasna (2016). "Reform of the royal Cambodian armed forces organization to meet the challenges of the 21st century," *Korean Journal of Defense Analysis* 28: 249–75.

Vasavakul, Thaveeporn (2001). "From revolutionary heroes to red entrepreneurs," in *Coercion and Governance: The Declining Political Role of the Military in Asia*, ed. Muthiah Alagappa. Stanford, CA: Stanford University Press, 336–56.

von der Mehden, Fred (1970). "The military and Thailand in development," *Journal of Comparative Administration* November: 323–40.

Walsh, Sean P. (2007). "The roar of the lion city: ethnicity, gender, and culture in the Singapore armed forces," *Armed Forces & Society* 33: 265–85.

Womack, Sarah (2009). "Ethnicity and martial races: the Garde indigene of Cambodia in the 1880s and 1890s," in *Colonial Armies in Southeast Asia*, ed. Karl Hack and Tobias Rettig, London: Routledge, 107–25.

Woo, Jongseok (2010). "Crafting democratic control of the miltiary in South Korea and the Philippines: the problem of military factions," *Contemporary Politics* 16: 369–82.

Woods, Kevin (2011). "Ceasefire capitalism: military–private partnerships, resource concessions and military–state building in the Burma–China borderlands," *Journal of Peasant Studies* 38: 747–70.

Wurfel, David (1988). *Filipino Politics: Development and Decay*. Ithaca, NY: Cornell University Press.

Wyatt, David K. (1984). *Thailand: A Short History*. New Haven and London: Yale University Press.

Yawnghwe, Chao-Tzang (1997). *The Politics of Authoritarianism: The State and Political Soldiers in Burma, Indonesia, and Thailand*. University of British Columbia: ProQuest Dissertations and Theses.

Cambridge Elements

Politics and Society in Southeast Asia

Edward Aspinall

Australian National University

Edward Aspinall is Professor of Politics at the Coral Bell School
of Asia-Pacific Affairs, Australian National University. A specialist of Southeast
Asia, especially Indonesia, much of his research has focused on democratization,
ethnic politics, and civil society in Indonesia and, most recently, clientelism
across Southeast Asia.

Meredith L. Weiss

University at Albany

Meredith L. Weiss is Professor of Political Science at the University at Albany,
SUNY. Her research addresses political mobilization and contention, the politics of
identity and development, and electoral politics in Southeast Asia, with particular
focus on Malaysia and Singapore.

About the Series

The Elements series Politics and Society in Southeast Asia includes
both country-specific and thematic studies on one of the world's most dynamic
regions. Each title, written by a leading scholar of that country or theme,
combines a succinct, comprehensive, up-to-date overview of debates
in the scholarly literature with original analysis and a clear argument.

Cambridge Elements ☰

Politics and Society in Southeast Asia

Elements in the Series

Politics, Political Economy and Identity Mobilization in Indonesia
Jamie Davidson

Civil–Military Relations in Southeast Asia
Aurel Croissant

A full series listing is available at www.cambridge.org/ESEA.

Printed in the United States
By Bookmasters